ECHOES OF A UNIVERSITY PRESIDENCY

SELECTED SPEECHES

BY J. DONALD MONAN, S.J.

Foreword by Geoffrey T. Boisi

Linden Lane Press at Boston College
Chestnut Hill, Massachusetts

Linden Lane Press at Boston College
140 Commonwealth Avenue
3 Lake Street Building
Chestnut Hill, Massachusetts 02467
617-552-4820
www.bc.edu/lindenlanepress

ISBN 978-0-9816416-2-1

Front cover: Portrait of J. Donald Monan, S.J., by Gary Wayne Gilbert

Printed in the USA

CONTENTS

CHAPTER V

HAPPENINGS ALONG THE WAY

O NE OF THE great privileges of my life has been to be a son of Boston College: as an alumnus, 25-year trustee, long-time member of the board's executive committee, and chairman of the board. More important to me, however, is that Boston College gave me the gift of the friendship and mentoring of J. Donald Monan, of the Society of Jesus.

I have had a ringside seat for a 24-year tenure of presidential leadership that encompassed what was perhaps the most complete transformation of a higher educational institution in the past half-century. Fr. Monan's combination of vision, leadership, executive, intellectual, and people skills matched those of anyone I have met in business or the nonprofit worlds. My admiration for him, however, was forged by the inspiring way he exercised his gifts, in the context of his Jesuit spirituality, serving God and the greater good.

As a 1969 graduate of the College, I had been eyewitness to the social upheavals that were part of the challenges Fr. Monan would later face. By the time he arrived as president in 1972, the University's reserves of financial means, spirit, and purpose were literally exhausted. He brought clarity of mission, inspirational leadership, strategic planning, and unfailing good judgment in identifying the steps needed to move forward. Perhaps most important, he utilized an unerring eye in assembling a team of exactly the right people to bring the vision to reality. He also possessed the motivational skills to create a culture of excellence, caring, and a sense of family. He motivated all connected to the University to invest at a deep and personal level in the creation of the modern Boston College.

Those who have had the privilege of hearing Fr. Monan speak know they will be treated to an inspiring, eloquent, insightful, pragmatic, thought-provoking, spiritually centered, intellectual, and logically constructed discussion on an important topic—impacting society and the human condition. His choice of teachable moments is as interesting and varied as the building blocks of the revitalized institution he created.

The following pages are not a memoir written at the conclusion of his 24 years as president. But, perhaps better than a reflection on years past, this selection of speeches will open to a larger audience some of the words and ideals through which Boston College found its authentic voice.

GEOFFREY T. BOISI
Chairman and Chief Executive Officer
Roundtable Investment Partners LLC

O N A B E A U T I F U L July morning in 1972, I was just leaving the Administration Building at LeMoyne College in Syracuse to drive to Canada on vacation. At that moment, my former secretary called after me that a Father Frank Mackin was telephoning from New York. Frank being a longtime friend, I accepted the call.

After a few pleasantries, Frank told me that the Trustees of Boston College would like me to consider being a candidate for their presidency. I told him that four years as academic dean and vice president had convinced me that I much preferred teaching and writing to managerial tasks. I had resigned the dean's position and was already on my way out the door on vacation before beginning a sabbatical to prepare to return to the classroom. Frank asked, "Where are you going?" When I told him Canada, he said, "I'll meet you in Montreal tomorrow morning."

A month later, I accepted appointment as 24th president of Boston College. In the course of that month, my personal preferences had not changed, but the importance and urgency of the Trustees' invitation left little doubt as to where "the greater good" lay—if, that is, the challenge could be successfully met. Fortunately, at the age of 48, I had had enough experience with every level of university life to recognize the many strands of that challenge but enough enterprise to allow me to undertake it.

Later in this book, I shall attempt to separate out some of the differing strands woven into that challenge. Poor financial systems and controls had brought the College to the brink of bankruptcy. The social upheavals over race and war and poverty that swept through almost every campus in the nation between 1968 and 1972 had dislocated the University's academic priorities and left chasms of suspicion and distrust between too many of its clienteles. And at Boston College, uncertainties and divergent interpretations of developments brought about in the Second Vatican Council became a further source of painful division.

Twenty-four years later, the College found itself facing prospects as auspicious as they had previously been menacing: In the place of negative net worth, a $600 million endowment and a string of 24 uninterrupted balanced budgets; 30 new or totally refurbished major University buildings; its undergraduate program among the top 40 in the country; all but one of its graduate schools ranked among the top 25; clarity of purpose as to what the College was about and a pervasive spirit of trust in carrying it out.

Transitions such as this do not happen spontaneously nor can they be altogether programmed in advance. I would like, therefore, to take a moment to mention here some of the less tractable factors that played a powerful role in the dramatic transformation that Boston College experienced over those two and a half decades: At every level of the University from trustee to new hires, exceptionally gifted men and women with unfaltering dedication to the best interests of the institution; in the face of countless tantalizing alternatives, good sense to foresee what would work and what would not; in every endeavor, a conscientious effort to exercise quality control; finally, unhurried patience for institutional change to take place. Obviously, not every member of the University possessed each of these qualities in the same degree. And yet, each of these qualities played such a visible part in the major developments within the University that, to my mind, they characterized the institution itself.

In accepting the presidency of Boston College, I was aware

of the many lists of activities, some of them humorous, created to describe the responsibilities of a modern-day university president. Fundraiser, scholar, diplomat, financier, manager, negotiator, academic. Although most list makers would include "university spokesman" or "communicator" as a presidential responsibility, not many would include "speechwriter." That function understandably is often delegated to another.

Nevertheless, throughout the 24 years I served as president of Boston College, I looked upon public speaking or oral communication to all manner of groups as one of my most important and, if truth be told, enjoyable responsibilities. But if delivering talks was enjoyable, composing them was not. Unlike many presidents, I found myself incapable of taking advantage of a speechwriter. At the end of those 24 years, I found that I had in my files some 300 carefully composed presentations that I had delivered to all manner of audience—to newly arrived freshmen and mature professional school students, on educational topics and issues of broad societal interest, at Faculty Convocations, at pre-Commencement galas and at building dedications, at award ceremonies for individual alumni, and regrettably, at funerals of alumni sons and daughters.

The following pages contain a selection of those public presentations. They are not technically a history of Boston College during that quarter century, nor are they a coherent expression of my own philosophy of higher education. And yet they do contain elements of history and no matter what the explicit topic or audience, inevitably convey something of my own outlook and perspective on a wide variety of aspects of University life. Readers who were in the audience for the delivery of the 24 Faculty Convocation talks and most of the annual "President's Circle" addresses will realize that I was unable to include them in this volume. Whether readers were in attendance for the delivery of some of these presentations or are reading them for the first time, I hope that they do contain recognizable echoes of a very exciting period in the history of Boston College.

J. DONALD MONAN, S.J.
October 2008

CHAPTER I

IDEAS THAT
SHAPE STONE AND STEEL

Introduction

THE PHYSICAL FEATURES of a university, like the bodily appearance of a person, have the power to express and to a certain degree shape the spirit and the ideals of the institution. They can and should be a source of pride and confidence and healthy aspiration.

In 1972, the handsome Gothic buildings that were the pride of the Chestnut Hill Campus were eroding from too-long deferred maintenance. If the student body were to expand its base from the Northeast to embrace the entire country, a large increase in student resident and dining facilities would be imperative. And years of budgetary constraints would have to be broken to assure wholeness to the University's academic offerings.

The following pages trace the dedicatory ceremonies for a number of major new buildings, and of totally renovated and expanded earlier buildings. Over time, these changes renewed the aesthetic beauty of the campus and provided the physical capability to improve and expand and make whole the education of a developing undergraduate and graduate community.

In addition to the restoration of our architectural treasures of Gasson and Devlin Halls and of Bapst Library, an entire family of nine new student residences arose on Lower Campus near enhanced facilities for intercollegiate and recreational athletics. Most importantly, the creation of O'Neill Library, of Robsham Theater, the McMullen Museum of Art, the Merkert Chemistry Center, and the Law Library complemented the enhancements of each of the other existing academic facilities. All these provided greater wholeness to the students' experience of University academic life.

But always shaping the stone and steel were people, some of whose names appear on these buildings, and whose personal stories are intertwined with the meanings of these dedications. Beyond the personal, each ceremony became the occasion to reflect upon the deeper purposes of higher education.

Silvio O. Conte Forum

February 18, 1989

> *In the entire history of Jesuit education,*
> *since the founding of our first lay college in Italy*
> *in 1548, learning has never been prized*
> *as a good only for itself—but as a critical ingredient*
> *of leadership for effective service to others.*

T HIS AFTERNOON'S STORY had many beginnings. It began in Pittsfield, Massachusetts, when a recent World War II veteran with football on his mind first spoke to Fr. Joseph Barrett about his desire to attend Boston College.

It began on a Saturday afternoon on Alumni Field, where McElroy Commons now stands, when a lineman's injury cut short the thoughts of athletic stardom.

It began on long afternoons in St. Mary's Hall when Fr. J. F. X. Murphy patiently tutored him in Latin to prepare him for an academic program at Boston College that his training in a vocational high school had seemed to place beyond his reach.

And today's story began in March 1983, in Washington, when I told this athlete, this student—Congressman Silvio O. Conte—that the University had begun planning a dramatic new athletic and convocation center that our Board of Trustees desired to name in his honor.

For the past six years, the entire campus community has watched in awe as workmen hoisted into place some of the most complex steel beams in Boston's inventory of buildings. Our teams of students have patiently traveled early, cold mornings to practice on outdoor rinks to play as the visiting team even for their home games. More recently, this building provided the setting for the General of the Society of Jesus to address the alumni of Boston College High School and Boston College on his first visit to campus. And here in this ample space, our University singers and orchestra joined the Jesuit faculty members who celebrated a liturgy to conclude Boston College's 125th anniversary.

It is thanks to many people that the dream of this handsome new building has now come fully true. This afternoon we assemble to celebrate the completion of our new forum, to express our gratitude to all of those who have provided the financial means and the artistry and the vast human effort that have brought it to reality. But we assemble first and foremost to dedicate the building—to provide it with the name that will mark its individuality within our family of buildings. From this date forward, it will be the Silvio O. Conte Forum of Boston College.

Those of you who have had the opportunity to tour the voluminous reaches of this building realize the wealth of purposes it will serve, from competitive sports to scholarly lectures, from concerts to liturgies and Commencement exercises—and playing host to our surrounding communities. Indeed, in the few short months since it opened, Conte Forum has begun to transform life outside the classroom as dramatically as our O'Neill Library has transformed what it means to be a student at Boston College.

In choosing the names for our buildings, Boston College obviously displays gratitude to the persons it honors. In the case of Silvio Conte, we do not stand alone in our gratitude. As President George H. W. Bush has just observed, the name of Silvio Conte in the United States Congress has become synonymous with concern for education, for the physical classrooms and libraries and laboratories where education takes place, and even more, for the tiny children and young men and women who simply could not gain an education without the financial assistance his leadership has made possible. That leadership has meant consistently swimming against the tide of his political-party family for the past eight years. But it is a measure of the respect his convictions win, that a new president recognizes Mr. Conte's accomplishments for education as a model for his own.

In naming the Silvio O. Conte Forum, Boston College is voicing more than gratitude, however deep. In this case, the University is expressing pride in a beloved son in whose career it sees the clear outline and features of its own ideals.

Throughout the history of Western culture, human knowledge and understanding, the fruits of education, have been recognized as goods in their own right, worth pursuing for their own sake. But in the entire history of Jesuit education, since the founding of our first lay college in Italy in 1548, learning has never been prized as a good *only* for itself—but as a critical ingredient of leadership for effective service to others.

As one writer put it, the thrust of Jesuit education from the beginning had a clear objective: forming Christian men equipped and eager to exercise leadership for the good of their own era. Or, as the Jesuit General expressed it recently, "Our teaching will be directed toward forming ... men and women for others ... whose ideal is that of service; who enrich their own personalities for the enrichment of others; whose horizons stretch out to their fellow man across the farthest national and international frontiers."

Learning and the personal search for knowledge are a University's most treasured legacy, but that knowledge and learning must not be allowed to become sterile. Knowledge is creative; it does not reach its full purpose unless it is taken beyond the University, into the family, the Church, the business world, and the chambers of government.

These are lofty ideas—perhaps for some, abstractions—but they explain what we are about this day.

The name of Silvio O. Conte inscribed over the entrance of this building will not recall athletic stardom, however much a thrilling gift that can be. But the name will say that for one man, the desire to compete was the door that opened up a college education and a law degree—and a lifelong career of public service. Without that desire and opportunity to compete, this young man's life would have had all the dignity and religious motivation and integrity and familial satisfaction of the father he admired so dearly. But our nation would have been the poorer, less human in its care for the weak, less energetic in pursuing the causes of disease, less solicitous to husband the blessings of our environment, less determined to assure that today's young people—in whom he sees his own face—would have the opportunity to receive the quality education that he enjoyed.

If Silvio had not had that desire to compete, everyone across this land who has come to know him would have been the poorer. For in his case, the *style* of leadership in service has been as important as the leadership itself. For Mr. Conte, affairs of state are always concerns of people, to be dealt with directly and with understanding, to be argued with eloquence and courage, and resolved with compassion and unstinting generosity.

Because Mr. Conte is a son of Boston College, our efforts to honor him are inevitably a way of doing honor to our own ideals. Yet every university realizes humbly that it does not begin the learning process nor bring it to its creative conclusion.

As a person whose entire education rests on decades of immersion in Latin literature, I share Silvio's intense pride in the sensibilities and largeness of soul he brought to his education from an Italian family. As his alma mater salutes him,

Virgil in his *Georgics* salutes another forebear, classic Italy, as a parent of bounteous produce and as an even more bounteous parent of men ("... *salve, magna parens frugum, Saturnia tellus, magna virum* ...").

Parents indeed can take pride, but we all recognize in the last analysis they cannot take credit. The story of the young man fresh from the war and prepared to return to his work as a machinist at General Electric, to the halls of Congress and accolades by the president of the United States, is a story of faith and hope and much love given and received. And it is a story of one thing more that Virgil captured in the fifth book of the *Aeneid*. In describing the race between four galleys of his own Italian forces, he identifies the source of the achievement of the boat seizing the victory with the classic words, "... *hos successus alit: possunt, quia posse videntur*" ("they have the power to succeed because they are convinced they can").

With faith, and hope, and much love given and received, and with the power to succeed because he knew he could, Silvio Conte is a person Boston College is proud to honor this day.

Silvio O. Conte (J.D. '49) died on February 8, 1991. The first President Bush, who styled himself as the "Education President," once called Conte the "Education Congressman." Running as a Republican in Massachusetts, Conte never lost an election in his 32-year career.

Bapst Reborn: Burns Library of Rare Books and Special Collections

April 22, 1986

*Great university libraries stand as testimony
to learning achieved. In a particular sense, special collections and
archives stand as testimony to the illuminating process of
knowledge itself, whose unremitting pursuit
is the university's mission.*

W E GATHER THIS afternoon surrounded by the breathtaking beauty of stained glass and Gothic towers and all manner of art that is wrought in wood and leather and colored fabric. And numerous as we are, we realize that we are not alone among these beauties. For this ceremony of dedication and rededication bridges time and links generations—within the Burns family, within the Jesuit family, and within the life of Boston College.

The ideals and hopes and dreams of great persons are all about us today. The dreams of Fr. Bapst and later presidents who first planned and laboriously placed stone upon stone; the generous hopes of a young alumnus, Judge John J. Burns, who deeply loved this library, and loved still more his young family, for whom he entertained such lofty hopes; the aspirations of a Margaret Ford, who appreciated the value of an education she had not been privileged to receive; and the patient care of a Terence and Brendan Connolly, whose discriminating judgment in beginning our early collections has been complemented by a former student who gained his appreciation of historic books in this building.

But if the seeds of today's accomplishments were sown in the early days of this century, their flowering in 1986 is the handiwork of many people present with us today. One cannot purchase the sensitivity and artfulness and care of our architects and builders. Those qualities must come from within, from the ideals and sensibilities of those who not only know good work, but find the source of their own pride in accomplishing it. Our provident trustees not only supervised every step of the planning; they generously provided resources— sometimes anonymously, sometimes in the names of admired friends—to execute the plans artfully. And what can be said of the family of Judge John J. Burns, of beloved wife and sons and daughters and spouses and grandchildren, who have expressed in their own maturity their love and gratitude and continuing admiration, by forever linking his name to a learned cause that he appreciated 40 years ago? Gabriel Marcel says that if you really love someone, you know that person will live forever. If love gives eyes to understand, the enduring love of the Burns family will make their father live for new generations of grandchildren, and for countless young men and women who will follow his footsteps as students at Boston College.

As I have gratitude to each of these, I have sincere pride in those members of the Boston College staff whose expertise and care have given new strength and beauty to this building as surely as the mortar that binds its stones.

Our dedication today brings to a successful and joyous conclusion a process of library rebuilding that has transformed the physical and technological features of the campus, and in the process has transformed what it means to be a student and a research scholar at Boston College. It is especially fitting that the last act in this recreative process be the rededication of our most beautiful work of Gothic art, and the dedication of the Burns Library of Rare Books and Special Collections.

If the heart of a university is its faculty, the books ranged on a library's shelves are its second faculty, revealing the insights and interpretations and accumulated wisdom of thinkers in ages past, and giving the clues that will fire young minds to create new meanings in the years ahead. But there is a special reason why a university should cherish its archives and give pride of place to its rare books and special collections. Throughout the history of Western thought, human intelligence has been described through the metaphor of light, and the grasp of meaning in the world around us has always been likened not to some form of passive absorption, but to the active process of illuminating darkness and letting meaning stand free.

The light of human intelligence is elusive. All libraries capture that light and preserve it. The special collections in our libraries, composed as they so often are, of manuscripts and tentative sketches and meeting notes and preliminary drafts, capture the process of illumination itself. For young minds, they bring to life the struggle and tentative formulations and insights that take place as meaning dawns for the great thinker or the diplomat, for the statesman or the jurist. Great university libraries stand as testimony to learning achieved. In a particular sense, special collections and archives stand as testimony to the illuminating process of knowledge itself, whose unremitting pursuit is the university's mission.

In his *Spiritual Exercises*, which formed the apostolic outlook of all future Jesuits, Ignatius of Loyola urged his followers to nourish the capacity to see God in all things. Eleven centuries earlier, in his monumental work on the Trinity, St. Augustine saw in the noblest functions of our human spirit, in our intelligence and its learning, in our hearts and their loves, no less than the image of God's own creative intelligence and love. Perhaps the clearest way of understanding this perspective is through the example of the stained glass window. Without the sun behind it, it stands dull and mute and opaque. It takes on the beauty of its own colors and brilliance only when it reveals a light that stands beyond it as a source of its meaning and beauty. This building has always been a monument to human learning; through the generosity of the Burns family, and of so many others with us today, it is in a new sense a monument to human love. As we dedicate and rededicate this noble building, my prayer is, in the spirit of Augustine and of Ignatius, that as the stained glass around us assumes its own fullest beauty when revealing a source beyond it, the wealth of human understanding and of human love that are invested and enshrined in this building will serve to reveal to new generations, not only the wonders of human intelligence, but the light of that creative intelligence, and the fire of that love, that are the source of all meaning.

Thomas P. O'Neill Jr. Library

October 14, 1984

*Leadership calls for power, and power carries
a potent magic to turn the heads of those
who hold it. The antidote to that magic lies in the
recognition we call gratitude, the recognition that our
most valuable traits are gifts to us.*

As the sun has risen over the Boston skyline for the past three years, I have been able to look out my residence window in St. Mary's to see this burgeoning building rise from the earth and assume the magnificent form that stands before us this afternoon. During those same years, students by the thousands filed longingly by the structure on their way from Lower Campus residences to their classrooms and laboratories in the striking Gothic buildings that surround our plaza. Their young eyes dreamed the same dream that three decades of Boston College students and faculty—and presidents—have dreamed: a research library to match the stature and aspirations of this fine university.

Thanks to many people, that dream has come true. This afternoon, we assemble to celebrate the completion of our library, to express our gratitude to all of those who have provided the financial means and the artistry and the vast human effort that have brought it to reality. But we assemble, also, to dedicate the building, to provide it with a name. From this day forward, it will be the Thomas P. O'Neill Jr. Library of Boston College.

In choosing names for our buildings, Boston College has obviously portrayed its admiration of the persons it has honored, but it has also displayed certain characteristics about itself, its religious character, its Jesuit origins, its indebtedness to friends. Yet among all university resources, a library plays a unique role, both in symbol and in reality. A great research library makes visible the fundamental mission of a university; it is the locale where young minds meet the great thinkers of all ages, not only to gain "vision" from the past, but also to gather the stimulus and the clues to a new knowledge that will dispel the puzzles of a new generation.

In other words, when Boston College chooses a name for its library, it says something about the purpose of the university itself, even about the purpose of human learning.

Despite all their importance, Boston College's paradigm academic building will not be named for a professorial scholar or an ecclesiastical figure or an imaginative dean. Instead, it will be named for a former student who, for 48 years, has exercised leadership in public service to people of every social station, of high estate and low, persons of power and of incredible fragility, among the world's most cultured nations, and among those for whom a simple school or simple meal are beyond their horizon.

Hundreds of literary portraits of Speaker O'Neill have appeared in books and journals and news media for the world's reading. The name inscribed in the granite of the Thomas P. O'Neill Jr. Library is addressed to our students and to students of all ages everywhere.

Among our more than 85,000 Boston College graduates, Thomas P. O'Neill has risen to the highest position of public service in our nation. But it is the manner in which he has exercised that leadership that is more the reason for our admiration and affection than is the degree of his prominence. In an era where the needs and problems of the human family are measured in anonymous millions and their solutions expressed only in statistical equations, Speaker O'Neill has always seen those needs in a single human face. Those of us who have lived through the decades since the '30s of dramatic change in the strength of family ties, in challenges to religious convictions, in the crises of wars and threats to peace, in the strains of civil strife and betrayal of government leadership—those of us who have lived through these changes realize that Speaker O'Neill's legendary sense of loyalty is no dull or wooden conformity. It has been a creative fidelity to values pledged in his youth that he kept relevant to a world in constant change by dint of effort and imagination and personal sacrifice.

In his style of leadership, Speaker O'Neill was never the scholarly specialist. He has been gifted rather with that unique combination of personal qualities that make leadership effective, the intuitive insight of what will work in complex situations; the clear sense of values as to what should be made to work in an arena of competing interests, and the strength or force of personality that can make things work when the surroundings are in confusion or in conflict.

Any educational system that proposes leadership as an ideal poses an implicit threat to its own graduates. Leadership calls for power, and power carries a potent magic to turn the heads of those who hold it. The antidote to that magic lies in the recognition we call gratitude, the recognition that our most valuable traits are gifts to us.

The Speaker lost his mother to tuberculosis when he was only a year old. But the term "Jr." carved in the name of Thomas P. O'Neill Jr. is permanent tribute of gratitude to a father who gave to the young family its sense of identity, its mutual love and cohesion.

For the person who knows his roots and is grateful, power is no danger. Like knowledge, it is another instrument of service to others. In the library, then, we have the symbol and the fruit of the University's search for wisdom.

In the Thomas P. O'Neill Jr. Library, we have a graduate's name that has become synonymous with leadership in public service. But there is a final link in the mission of Boston College and in the life of Speaker O'Neill that binds wisdom and service together in a unique way.

As early as Genesis, and in all the wisdom literature of the Hebrew Testament, wisdom is portrayed as God's helpmate and companion in the creation of our world. And in John's gospel the Word who is Wisdom reappears—this time as a person but also as the power that expresses God's intent and carries creation forward through a new manifestation of love for mankind. The story of Genesis, the story of the Christian faith that we believe, is that creation is not ended. There is a new earth and a new heaven that awaits our building. It is the role of the university, with its wisdom and with the creative leadership of its graduates, to help make sure that the culture we create will be of benefit to all mankind.

Thomas "Tip" O'Neill Jr. died on January 5, 1994. While still a senior at Boston College in 1935, he ran for the Cambridge City Council—the first and only loss of his legendary political career. His papers are maintained in the Boston College Burns Library of Rare Books and Special Collections.

The Wallace E. Carroll
School of Management
March 18, 1989

*From its role in creating the conditions of a life of dignity
and sufficiency, American business in the past
50 years has increasingly gained influence in shaping
the outlines themselves of what human
aspirations should be.*

Boston college knows very well, from the experience of recent years, that anniversaries are occasions to pause—and to look back. In our case, the return to our history has been reason for much spontaneous thanksgiving—the 60th anniversary of our Law School, the 40th of Nursing, and 50th of the Graduate School of Social Work—and last year the 125th anniversary of the University itself.

There are two features of the 50th anniversary of the School of Management, however, that set it apart. Oh, indeed, there is, as with the other schools of the University, abundant reason for thanksgiving to the men and women who gave it growth and stature—for the young lives the school helped form through its faculty and for the respect their professionalism and integrity reflected back upon their alma mater.

During the 50-year lifetime of the School of Management, however, the very intellectual disciplines that drive the management process have been transformed. The management of the world's business has increasingly become a technical science as well as an art. Even more importantly, business has carved out its own place beside law and government and education and communications and technology as one of the great formative forces within culture itself. From its role in creating the conditions of a life of dignity and sufficiency, American business in the past 50 years has increasingly gained influence in shaping the outlines themselves of what human aspirations should be.

But with influence and leadership come new responsibilities to assure that the culture business is helping to shape genuinely enriches the human family—and families—not impoverish them. Business finally knows as its own the frightening responsibility of every teacher within society— to assure that the web of values and of relationships it creates nourish the human spirit as well as its material needs—and that the professions it makes desirable to the most imaginative and talented among our young be worthy of their very best selves.

If Boston College did not possess a school of management, it would have to create one in order to be true to the aspiration of Jesuit education, to reach those who are leaders in each contemporary generation. Fortunately, we can today look back to a record in which our School of Management was an important participant in the transformation of business education and in the role that business itself has assumed in our society. But thanks to the generosity and dedication of one of our graduates whose career spans the dramatic changes of the past 50 years, today is not just an anniversary. It is a new beginning of The Wallace E. Carroll School of Management at Boston College.

The conferral of a new name means the assumption of a new identity. The identity of Wallace Carroll and the identity of the School of Management are not captured in a record of dates and events and transactions. Identity and character lie more in the ideals to which we aspire as we weave a pattern of events and accomplishments in our lives.

The fact that Wallace Carroll is not with us today is a measure of the modesty of this distinguished man. Sixty years an alumnus of Boston College, he enjoys the vigor and the keenness of mind that have been his gifts of a lifetime. If the school were being named in honor of his mother and father, as Wallace originally desired, I am sure that he would be on this platform this afternoon. But while I was able to persuade him of the educational advantages of identifying the school with an individual alumnus, his characteristic reluctance to accept personal honors or praise remained unchanged.

I spoke to Wallace yesterday, however, and he sent a little message:

"I am sorry I cannot be with you today but wish to express my deepest appreciation for the honor being bestowed on the Carroll family. What we have contributed to Boston College is only a small measure of what Boston College has done for us and the sons and daughters of Ireland and other ethnic groups over the past 125 years. Boston College has become one of the great Catholic universities and we are honored to have our name as part of the School of Management."

Wallace E. Carroll was the first alumnus I met upon assuming the presidency of Boston College. Two days before my arrival on campus, Wallace came East to begin this acquaintance. For two decades before, however, he had been an advisor and strong support to three previous presidents. The devotion to Boston College that made it an integral part of his life showed itself in the welcomes he and Le extended to young alumni beginning their careers in Chicago, to cross-country telephone broadcasts of Boston College athletic events, to a significant leadership role—until today an anonymous role—in every major fundraising effort the University has undertaken. Boston College owes much gratitude to Wallace Carroll and to Le who has extended her hospitality and shared our fortunes for decades, and to the family, that so clearly are heirs of their profound dedication to Boston College.

But in permitting us to forge this new association of the name of Wallace E. Carroll and the School of Management, Wallace has enriched the school in an entirely new way. He has given us a new source of pride. Wallace was perhaps the first Boston College graduate to fashion a leadership role in a conglomerate business whose reach extends from Eastern Europe to the Far East. Wallace did not assume command of a ship that was already afloat. He assembled it plank by plank while the winds shifted around him and while newly recruited hands needed an inspiration they could trust, as much as they needed professionally sound direction and results.

The record of Wallace's business acumen, of his courage and judgment, is written on the pages of his business career. The motives that urged him have to be inferred from the actions rather than the words of this strong but reticent man. Wallace's business associates are his circle of personal friends. His weekends away from the office are occasions to develop personal and family familiarities with company colleagues. His imposing financial success has left him both as appreciative of and as detached from material goods as in his student days when he worked as a telephone operator in St. Mary's Hall in return for his room in Philomathia Hall.

Most of all, Wallace is a person for whom ownership is stewardship; who is steward, and steward only, of his extraordinary resources. He is a person who expects to be asked because he understands he is there to help.

Wallace Carroll's business career had its start at almost the same time as the School of Management was founded. He witnessed and helped create within the marketplace the transformation in the intellectual discipline and in the cultural importance of American business. I trust that the ideals he gained at Boston College and took to the world's marketplace will serve to enrich in a new way our educational process and the careers of our graduates. It is with great pride and gratitude that I today establish the new name of The Wallace E. Carroll School of Management.

Wallace E. Carroll commuted to Boston College from his home in Taunton and graduated in 1928. He attended Harvard Business School and shortly thereafter moved to Chicago, where he assembled and served as chairman and CEO of the conglomerate Katy Industries. Through their influential presence in Chicago and Florida, Wallace and his wife Le introduced the College and its graduates to those locales. Wallace continued his lifelong dedication to Boston College, serving on its Board of Directors and Board of Trustees until his death on October 1, 1990.

Merkert Chemistry Center

April 24, 1992

*High-minded men and women, not scientists themselves,
have always been willing to step forward, to provide
the means for scientists and scholars to carry their investigations
wherever the brilliance of their imagination took them.*

T HIS ARRAY OF splendid laboratories and of sophisticated instruments are centuries in advance of those within
the venerable walls of the first university at Bologna or of the
stately buildings at Oxford or Paris. Yet, in our gathering we
reenact the central theme of the university's history within
the life of the human family. We gather as scholars and students, as artisans and builders, as generous men and women
philanthropists, conscious that out of our combined efforts
the institution we call the university is able to advance the
culture of our human family.

Students and scholars have always been dependent in their
work on generous men and women who believed in the importance of what they were about. High-minded men and
women, not scientists themselves, have always been willing to step forward, to provide the means for scientists and
scholars to carry their investigations wherever the brilliance
of their imagination took them. The surest proof that scholars and scientists and students have used their freedom re-
sponsibly and merited the trust placed in them is the story
of the cultural transformation all of us have witnessed in our
lives. This afternoon assures that the story of the University

in the world's culture continues to be written.

Ladies and gentlemen, the hopes and aspirations of many individuals are expressed in the stone and steel of this building. As we dedicate it, I want to pay special tribute to Dr. Jeong-Long Lin and Dr. David McFadden and their associates in the chemistry department whose experience as scientists brought the building from its first faint hopes to its present reality.

Most of all, however, I am grateful to all those generous individuals whose names are now permanently inscribed throughout these corridors and classrooms. It is, after all, your generosity that made possible the entire enterprise.

We have reserved a special mark of gratitude to Mr. Eugene F. Merkert. In choosing names for buildings, Boston College has obviously portrayed its admiration of the persons it has honored. But in dedicating a building, we also wish to provide it with a name that will mark its individuality within our family of buildings as surely as a personal name marks each of us. From this day forward, it will be the Eugene F. Merkert Chemistry Center.

The scientific work that takes place in this center will mirror the accomplishments of Gene Merkert's extraordinary business career because they are the marks of his person and his character: gifted talent and originality, initiative and unflinching hard work, challenge and energetic drive—and humility, both in setback and in brilliant success.

Many individuals have left their mark on the physical outlines and contour of this handsome center. In dedicating this structure as the Eugene F. Merkert Chemistry Center, it is my hope that Gene's originality and his humble, but determined sense of purpose will herald its spirit and capture the personality of the scientific work that is accomplished here.

Eugene F. Merkert was born on Long Island in New York on August 13, 1918. Due to very limited resources, Gene was obliged to begin work early in life to assist his mother in meeting family expenses, but eventually succeeded in attending NYU. Gene spent the whole of his life in the food brokerage business, where success depended as much on personal trustworthiness as on professionalized techniques. In founding and leading Merkert Enterprises, Gene became one of the nation's largest and most influential brokers of frozen foods before diversifying into other science-based businesses.

Naming The E. Paul Robsham Jr. Theater Arts Center

October 25, 1985

> *We measure the worth of people not by what*
> *they have done, but by who they are. And it is love that*
> *opens eyes to see who each individual is.*

Ladies and gentlemen, we are gathered here this evening for a ceremony that will profoundly mark the personality of this Theater Arts Center. We have gathered to confer upon this building its own proper name.

The tradition of naming university buildings is almost as old as the university tradition itself. In the majority of cases, the names conferred are those of individuals who have made their mark among us with long careers of brilliant accomplishments. Often enough, the name recognizes the very person whose generosity called the building into existence. In naming the O'Neill Library, the soaring towers of Gasson Hall, the stately beauty of Lyons Hall, Boston College recognized men who had employed their abundant length of days in remarkable deeds that won deserved admiration and even, perhaps, a certain awe.

But this is Parents Weekend at Boston College—a period when the entire University is able to look through the eyes of mothers and fathers and know again that if its buildings were brought about by mature men and women of accomplishment, they all *exist* for young people, they exist for our students.

Therefore, it is especially appropriate that tonight, for the first time, the College has the happiness of dedicating one of its educational facilities in the name of a student. We measure the worth of people not by what they have done, but by who they are. And it is love that opens eyes to see who each individual is. We name the Theater Arts Center in honor of E. Paul Robsham Jr. because of who he was—a valued student of Boston College, and a beloved son to his mother and father.

All of us who are here this evening are friends of Paul and Joyce. We see through their eyes and feel through their hearts what they too are accomplishing this evening. In this ceremony of dedication, Boston College lends its voice to give permanent, tangible expression to a love that each of you share, and that Boston College shares for one of its students.

E. Paul Robsham Jr. entered Boston College in the fall of 1982 after graduating from Belmont Hill High School. In addition to his assiduous schoolwork through middle and high school, Paul had proven his dedication and enjoyment of sports through years of action as a goalie in hockey. Paul tragically lost his life in an automobile accident a week after the close of class on May 23, 1983.

Dedicating the Boston College Theater Arts Center

October 30, 1981

"Camelot" is built upon the Arthurian legend
that has for so many centuries reflected our human quest
for perfection and our all too human shortcomings
in the course of that quest.

T ONIGHT, WE PRESENT the timeless story, *Camelot*.
Tonight, our own theater program has achieved its own kind
of *Camelot*.

At last we have a superb instrument for teaching and learning in the performing arts, whose values Jesuits have inte-
grated into their curricula for more than 400 years, for the
last 116 years here at Boston College.

We stand tonight, then, in a long tradition of other stages
in other Jesuit colleges that nurtured some of the great artists
in Western civilization, from the 17th-century Spanish Cal-
deron and De Vega to the great French playwright Moliere, to
somewhat more familiar names for most of us, like Charles
Laughton and Alfred Hitchcock. Only last night, Washington's Kennedy Center opened a new play entitled *Kingdoms*
that was written by an alumnus of the class of 1952, Mr. Edward Sheehan.

Recalling names I have just mentioned, one could easily
conclude that a great college needs only three rooms—a classroom, a library, and a theater. The theater because neither

the spoken work of the teacher, nor the brilliance captured in libraries, can equal the graphic power of theater to make an audience look beyond its own world, to see and feel and actually enter the world experienced by great playwrights. On this stage, the poetic worlds of Shakespeare and Chekhov and O'Neill will come to life again.

There is, I think, great felicity in the production chosen to inaugurate our beautiful new theater arts center. *Camelot* is built upon the Arthurian legend that has for so many centuries reflected our human quest for perfection and our all too human shortcomings in the course of that quest. *Camelot* is also an outstanding example of one of America's most original contributions to theater, the musical drama. And we are indeed fortunate to have in the leading role tonight one of the stars of the musical theater who for decades has personified excellence in his profession, Mr. Gordon MacRae.

I should perhaps also add that for Bostonians, the image of *Camelot* will forever conjure up the high-hearted aspirations of a young man born in this city, and an honorary alumnus of this institution who achieved the presidency of the United States.

But at last the time for remembering and planning and building, and even giving thanks, has come to a close. To borrow from another musical, it is literally time to "go on with the show."

Athletic and Convocation Center
June 12, 1986

You have experienced through athletics the
personal development of those qualities of self-confidence, an
understanding of what it means to lead and
what it means to cooperate with others who are leading,
the capacity to undergo hardship.

I T I S A great pleasure for me to extend a welcome and a very sincere word of gratitude to all of you for your presence here this afternoon. Your enthusiasm and your large numbers reflect the great importance of the project that we are about to undertake. Our new Sports Center is going to be important not only in terms of the financial commitment we will be making; the financial commitment also reflects the importance that the center is going to have both to our intercollegiate athletic programs, to the life of the University, and in a very genuine sense, I believe, to the life of the wider community.

Of all the new buildings recently erected on campus, the three that promise the most distinctive contribution are our new research library, our performing arts theater, and now this Sports and Convocation Center that we are about to begin. Together, they reflect the academic life of the institution, the cultural life of the institution, and the athletic aspirations that have been so much a part of the spirit of Boston College and of its striving for excellence.

Among all of you in attendance today, trustees, friends of

the University, those who once proudly played on Boston College teams, members of the larger community, I trust there is no need to recount the important role that athletic programs have played not only in Boston College education, but in American education generally. All of us realize the primacy of the academic within the mission of every college and university, and yet there is an element of the educational enterprise that is even more difficult to impart than that of the strictly academic disciplines. That element is the development of those personal qualities that are so important in life beyond the academic instruction that one can get from a book or a laboratory or a teacher. All of you who have participated in sports have recognized athletics as a vehicle for that type of education. You have experienced through athletics the personal development of those qualities of self-confidence, an understanding of what it means to lead and what it means to cooperate with others who are leading, the capacity to undergo hardship, the capacity to have perspective on what is important and what is less important, the capacity to make judgments and instant decisions as to what will work, the courage that is necessary to face adversity as well as to experience victory, the capacity to understand what it means to invest your emotions deeply in a cause, and yet not so deeply that they completely dominate you. While the communication of these personal qualities that are so important to adult life is the goal of all extracurricular activities, varsity sports provide a unique vehicle for their development.

There is another reason, however, why we should be enthusiastic about the creation of this particular building. We tend to identify great cities and great institutions with distinctive examples of architecture. Boston has been symbolized from coast to coast by the John Hancock Tower. And Boston College has long had for our architectural signature the towers on the Heights—Gasson Tower and the Ford Tower of Bapst

Library—and that will always be the case. Nevertheless, there is another set of buildings, McHugh Forum-Roberts Center, that have had a distinctive role in the history of Boston College because they have been the doorway for children in the neighborhood, for exciting exploits of student-athletes and for graduates of Boston College, always to return. The new Sports Center that we are creating is never going to replace the symbolic or the substantive importance of an O'Neill Library, of a Gasson Tower or a Bapst. But it is my fond hope that this building is going to continue to be that doorway to the neighborhood children, to our graduates, to the friends of the University—the first doorway, perhaps, that many of them will enter, but one that is only a doorway to all of the enormous intellectual and cultural and religious resources that have been the source of pride of Boston College.

Flynn Rec Plex

October 14, 1979

*All of us have learned from sports our
interdependence on each other, how to cooperate with each other,
the difficult lessons of how to win and how to lose.*

W E ARE CONDUCTING two ceremonial events today;
the first is the formal naming of this William J. Flynn Student Recreation Complex. The second is a testimonial to Bill
himself, later in the evening.

Since I will have an opportunity at the testimonial to say
a few personal words about Bill, I am going to spare him the
embarrassment of twice being a target for my rhetoric, and
take these few moments rather to talk about the role of athletics within the life of this University.

There are universities that are embarrassed about their
athletic programs—either because the magnitude of their
commitment distorts public understanding of their academic ambitions, or still worse, because they fear that the energies needed to fuel their programs actually run counter to
the educational goals they publicly profess. Any university
with a major varsity intercollegiate program must periodically test whether any worries it may have from these quarters are legitimate. What is not legitimate for a university is
to question its commitment to athletics and other physical
forms of recreation simply because they are physical.

Apart from swimming, this building, as you know, is totally devoted to nonvarsity athletics and recreation. Of the

12,000 students and staff who use it every week, almost exactly one-half are women. I consider the vast array of activities that take place in this complex a genuine addition to the educational experience of our students.

I believe this, not just because many of the sports organized here are actually taught by instructors. Much learning, of all sorts, takes place without benefit of an instructor. For young people, experience itself can be immensely educational—an Arthur Fiedler concert on the Esplanade, a Papal motorcade in the rain, a field goal six inches outside the uprights with 15 seconds left on the clock.

All of us have learned from sports our interdependence on each other, how to cooperate with each other, the difficult lessons of how to win and how to lose. Even more importantly, sports are today one of the few avenues for young people to gain familiarity with human strength and physical force—to learn to respect strength and power not as something evil, but for what they can accomplish; and to know as well that they can be abused.

The fact that our women students use the Flynn Complex as frequently as do our men has special educational importance to Boston College.

Many years in all-male and coeducational classrooms have taught me that if women's contribution to political life and business life and the academy is not as extensive as that of men, it is not for lack of talent, or judgment, or intellectual accomplishment on the part of women. One reason, I believe, is the more fragile sense of self-confidence that young women too often experience as they come to maturity. Lack of self-confidence is a notorious brake on talent. It is my hope that today's increased enjoyment and proficiency and success in sports will assist many young women to grow to a degree of self-confidence that will further liberate their extensive talents.

The buildings of our fine campus bear proud names of col-

lege founders and Cardinal Archbishops, of deans and benefactors. Naming the buildings in their honor expressed the
University's respect and admiration and gratitude for what
they contributed to Boston College. So it is with the William
J. Flynn Student Recreation Complex. But there is more. In
affixing his name to this building, we express the hope that
his integrity and dedication, his strength and understanding,
his unrelenting love for Boston College people and for its ideals, will belong to all of us.

Gabelli Hall

December 13, 1995

*Insofar as this residence bears the name of a
Boston College parent, it will speak to each of its residents about
his or her unique importance within their own families.*

T HIS IS A celebration day that has long been delayed. It was slightly more than 10 years ago that we began to plan the creation of the two residence halls here on Commonwealth Avenue. In fashioning that plan, we were quite obviously aware of the fact these would be prime buildings fronting on Commonwealth Avenue, and should appropriately contribute to the décor of our beautiful city. Consequently, we wanted to make sure that they would be architecturally elegant, that they would echo some of the Gothic elements of our main campus buildings, that they would be in their interior commodious and of the highest quality of construction. I think we were successful in meeting all of those aspirations.

However, there has still been one thing lacking in this building. Since 1988, we have been referring to it by its number on Commonwealth Avenue. And the use of numbers, whether they be Social Security numbers or the dog tags of a person in the military, is too often a mark of impersonality. Today, for the first time, Gabelli Hall takes on the character of a full member of the University with its proper name and with a distinctive personality—a personality that visually communicates the College's youthful ambitions and its respect for quality even to those who pass by but do not have the opportunity to enter the campus and visit our earlier Gothic buildings.

Even more importantly, as a student residence, this building will speak to students. It will speak to students of the aspirations we have for them. But insofar as this residence bears the name of a Boston College parent, it will speak to each of its residents about his or her unique importance within their own families. And I hope it will speak to each of us of Mario Gabelli's deep but demanding concern for young people and his sense of the importance of higher education in their lives.

In years past, some of our earliest residences were named in honor of Jesuit saints, of former archbishops of the Archdiocese of Boston. We are so proud today that three of our residence halls are named for parents of Boston College students. When students choose to attend Boston College, their choice extends the aspirations of their parents, not only for their intellectual growth but for their growth into fully responsible adulthood. So much of the assimilation of values and of the personal development and psychological maturation of students takes place in the setting of student residences. It is more than fitting then that Gabelli Hall joins two other of our student residences in bearing the name of parents of Boston College students.

Vanderslice Hall

November 17, 1995

*Our residence halls are in every sense of the word
educational buildings, because so much of the development
to full maturity takes place in the growth that occurs
in our residence halls.*

W HEN VISITING A newly married couple who have just had their first child, the first question we normally ask is, "What is his or her name?" Names confer identity, convey the personality of the individual. The naming of buildings plays a similar role and amply merits a festive celebration. I am greatly pleased that all of you are with us today as we officially name this building the Joseph and Mae Vanderslice Hall. We had the privilege once before of naming a building in honor of parents of students. On this occasion, we reach back another generation to name a building after persons who are not only the parents of three graduates of Boston College, but are also grandparents of students as well.

When we give a name to this building, of course, we speak to many audiences. The building, situated here at the gate of Lower Campus, will speak to everyone who enters this campus. It will speak in the architectural beauty of line and of color, in the language of the beauty of architecture to all those who come here. But in a very special way, the building will speak with its name to students. We normally think of the educational buildings of a university as its classrooms and laboratory buildings. And yet in a very genuine sense, our residence halls are in every sense of the word educational buildings, because so much of the development to full maturity takes place in the growth that occurs in our residence halls.

It is especially appropriate that this building was designed primarily as the home of sophomore students. In the many years I taught, I always had a preference to teach sophomores. There is no year during college where the rate of growth to full maturity is more rapid than during the second year of college or university. People who enter sophomore year are very different persons when they leave nine months later. This building, therefore, will be a transitional building in many senses, especially in encouraging the educational development of our students here at the University.

I did not have the privilege of knowing Joseph and Mae Vanderslice. And yet there are two characteristics I am sure that were theirs that make their names ideal for a university building. As the parents of three sons who graduated from Boston College and then went on to gain their doctoral degrees, I am sure that Joseph and Mae Vanderslice had a thorough understanding of young people and a capacity to inspire them with the value and importance of education and of learning. I think for that reason it is especially appropriate that their names grace this hall.

Finally, of course, the names of this building speak to all of us about Tom and Peggy Vanderslice themselves, whose generosity made this building possible. Today we inscribe in stone a recollection of their regular acts of generosity toward the University that have been taking place for decades.

Several years ago I had the privilege of awarding an honorary doctoral degree to Rose Kennedy, at approximately the age of 90. Although we did not expect that she was going to speak, Mrs. Kennedy spontaneously rose to her feet. Her first words were to express her gratitude for what a wonderful mother and father she had had. I considered it a remarkable testimonial both to her and to her parents that when being honored at the age of 90, the first thing that came to her mind was her parents. As we attempt to honor Tom and Peggy today, it is a tribute to them that what they want us to do is direct our attention to Joseph and Mae Vanderslice, Tom's parents. So, Tom and Peggy, our very sincere gratitude for what you have done and for the marvelous testimony of your own feelings today.

Walsh Hall

October 2, 1982

From the days of the earliest Jesuit colleges
in the 16th century, boarding students were always referred
to in the official documents of the Society of Jesus as
"familiares"—as members of the family.

T ODAY'S CEREMONY IS one of two ways in which Boston College expresses its admiration and gratitude to one of our great personalities.

The language we use to express our admiration—the establishment of a professorial chair in bioethics and today's dedication of this handsome student residence—are efforts to communicate for all future time the University's sentiments toward Fr. Michael Walsh. The idiom we employ is also meant to illustrate some of the facets of the success of the person that we honor.

Here among Fr. Walsh's family, his faculty friends, his brother Jesuits, his fellow trustees, and among the residents of this building, there is certainly no need to restate the chronology of Fr. Walsh's life or even to retell the story of his monumental contributions to his alma mater as faculty member, as premedical advisor, as president, as trustee. The plaque, however, that we shall affix on the southwest wall of this building expresses that contribution very briefly in these words:

"Rev. Michael P. Walsh, S.J.—22nd President of Boston College. Father Michael P. Walsh was a builder—of faculty, of academic programs, of the student body, and of campus facilities. During his presidency he initiated the creation of six student residences and five major academic buildings. His accomplishments established him as architect of Boston College's transition from college to university."

In all that he did in his priestly ministry, Fr. Walsh was a thoroughgoing university person. His career and all of his striving were expressions of the nobility and the grandeur of the university tradition itself.

The university, of course, plays a very unique role in society. For if we as families and as businesses benefit from learning and enjoy rich art forms and put new skills and technology to work, it is the university whose mission it is to create all of these and to help shape culture. The university assists the human family to continually expand its horizons, to stretch its intelligence, to attempt new experiments, and to fashion new art forms. For this reason, the university has to be perfectionist. It has to constantly surpass the shortcomings in the knowledge and culture of every age and stimulate its students to reach upward to new ideals.

In all he did as a university person—as a faculty member and a president and trustee of a score of institutions—Fr. Walsh was relentless in stimulating universities to excellence. Nevertheless, what is most characteristic in our memories of Fr. Walsh was not his passion for excellence. There is complexity to every one of us human beings, and yet I think for most of us there is some single gestalt or impression we convey as we meet other people. In Fr. Walsh's case, it was not the objectivity of the scientist or the detachedness of an administrator, or the passion of a leader that struck us. It was rather the understanding and humility and helpfulness of a priestly friend. Indeed, he was a friend to everyone he met.

If he had a great passion for excellence and for the furthering of culture—and he did—he always saw culture as secondary to the human persons whom he served. Education for Fr. Walsh was an intensely personal enterprise in the sense that, for all of its rigor and nobility, education was meant to enhance the lives of individual people. That view of education is one of the reasons why it is so appropriate that his name grace this handsome residence hall.

The Jesuit tradition of education has always been a rigorous one, with excellence and the greater good as the watchwords. Still, from the days of the earliest Jesuit colleges in the 16th century, boarding students were always referred to in the official documents of the Society of Jesus as *"familiares"*—as members of the family. "Members of the family"—words that connote students' need for understanding and support that a family atmosphere provides.

It is Fr. Michael P. Walsh's passion for excellence and his understanding and support and concern for the growth of individual students that make this an ideal setting to honor his name.

Reverend Michael P. Walsh, S.J., was born in South Boston on February 28, 1912, and became a Jesuit after graduating from Boston College High School. A research biologist, Fr. Walsh was a renowned advisor to medical and premedical students and was chairman of the biology department from 1948 to 1958, when he was named 22nd president of Boston College. During the years of his presidency from 1958 to 1968, Fr. Walsh refocused the College's energies on graduate education and research in order to enhance its university status. After retiring from Boston College, he served as president of Fordham University before returning to Boston, where he passed away on April 23, 1982.

Ignacio Hall

September 27, 1990

*With the blessing of the building that I will now
perform, it is with the prayer that the eloquence not of
their deaths, but that the eloquence of their lives, will always
speak to this University and speak to the students
of Boston College who will reside here.*

T HIS IS AN occasion that is both solemn and joyful. It is solemn, indeed, because of the persons whose memories we recall, and it is joyful because of the message that it contains for our University and for our students. Today we are dedicating a student residence in honor of two young women and six Jesuits who were slain on November 16, a year ago, on the campus of the Jesuit University in El Salvador. We have chosen the name "Ignacio" because it is the name of the person who was most eloquently the spokesman of the ideals that all of them stood for, and at the same time echoes the name of Ignatius Loyola, the founder of the group to which all of them belonged or were so closely attached—the founder of the order whose 450 years of life we begin to celebrate today.

I am sure that all of us realize that among the world's venerable institutions, universities have a special place of honor and of veneration. And so surely our eight martyrs—whether the distinguished scholar, Martin Baro, or the youthful child, Celina Ramos—all of them would consider it a wonderful honor to have their names recorded on a university building.

And yet the act of naming a university residence is not simply an honor to others; it is essentially to convey a message, a message to the university, a message of admiration of the people whose lives we celebrate, and a message of inspiration, both to the university and to the young men and women who will reside here. They have a message for us precisely because their deaths resulted from their ceaseless efforts to learn the truth and to speak the truth about their society—to speak the truth as human beings, as scholars, as teachers, as lecturers, as writers, to speak a truth about the pervasive impoverishment and repression and violence that was being done to their people. And in speaking that truth, they were perceived as threats to the military power, and as a result they suffered the consequences. But their message for us as a university is that they did tell the truth about the reality about them. They told it courageously, because they were repeatedly threatened, not only physically but also with bombs and with gunfire, before their final act of killing. They pursued the truth painstakingly, with all of the scholarship they could bring to their efforts, and they pursued it ceaselessly, seven days a week, without sabbaticals, for years and years. Perhaps most importantly, they pursued the truth in a spirit of service to their people. Scholars though they were, they recognized that truth has a larger purpose in society than its own, that it can serve as a constructive element to improve the conditions of the human family. Their efforts, therefore, at finding the truth as a way of service, were motivated ultimately by their compassion and by their profound Christian love for the people whom they attempted to serve.

The word "service" can be deceptive, because the service that they performed on behalf of the people of El Salvador was also a form of leadership. And indeed, universities and university people and graduates of universities who share that same sense of service, share that same sense and obligation of leadership.

Today, then, really is a solemn day, but a joyful day, because of the message that comes to us as a university and to our students. Perhaps it is most solemn because although the entire world lost the treasures of great scholars and humane Christian people, it was the poor of El Salvador who suffered the greatest loss, who are more defenseless because of their absence. Despite the solemnity, this occasion is also joyful, because in a sense their deaths gave dramatic eloquence and gave permanence to their lives. We are here today to testify to the permanence of their commitment, and with the blessing of the building that I will now perform, it is with the prayer that the eloquence not of their deaths, but that the eloquence of their lives, will always speak to this University and speak to the students of Boston College who will reside here.

Blessing Of Ignacio Hall

GOD, OUR FATHER, we gather here this morning at the start of the Ignatian year commemorating the founding of the Society of Jesus with gratitude for the rich heritage that gives Boston College its distinctive character. We pray that the name Ignacio Hall that now graces this residence may be a constant reminder of the lives of the six Jesuits and their two co-workers—men and women for others—sacrificed in the service of truth and the quest for justice. We pray that for all who live here, this name, "Ignacio," may be a challenge to emulation of the faith and courage that inspired their dedication to the life of the mind and the relief of human suffering. We ask You to bless all who live here with energy and enthusiasm for accomplishments of mind and heart, seeking, as Ignatius did, "in all things to love and to serve." Finally, we ask You, Lord, to bless Ignacio Hall with Your presence, to be always here among us with Your goodness and Your grace.

For all of this, we pray in the name of Jesus Christ, Your Son, our Lord. Amen.

The Jesuits were six of over 70,000 victims who died during El Salvador's civil war that raged during the 1980s and early 1990s. The vast majority were civilians killed at the hands of the armed forces and paramilitary death squads.

Greetings—Farewell: 28 Years of McHugh Forum

April 5, 1986

*There are so many people here tonight who, as
neighborhood children, had their first halting steps
on the ice in this building.*

T HIS HAS BEEN a very special night.

It is a special night for two reasons. One, it gives us the opportunity to express our congratulations and our thanks to this year's team, but especially to the team's graduating seniors. Certainly they have represented Boston College in a superb fashion, and, incidentally, I think they have proved it is not always the best team that wins the game. In hockey as perhaps in no other game, sometimes you can outplay an opponent and still come out on the short end of the score. But everyone associated with the University has been profoundly proud of what all of you have meant to the school, and proud of the way you have represented Boston College on the ice, in the classroom, and in the community.

It is also a very special night because it is our farewell to McHugh Forum. Not a sad farewell, despite the nostalgia, but a farewell of celebration for all it has meant to so many of us. Each of our two great coaches spent 14 years of their coaching careers in this building. There are so many people here tonight who, as neighborhood children, had their first halting steps on the ice in this building. And what it has meant to the alumni and friends and fans of the teams, who have shared the excitement and the disappointment of wins and losses throughout the years. And what it has meant to the team members themselves, as they have perspired through weeks and months of practices and through the triumphs and victories and some of the sadness of their losses. But especially what it has meant to our two coaches: to Len Ceglarski, who returned to Boston College as an alumnus to extend the magnificent coaching career that he had begun elsewhere, but continued here with his 500th, now his 535th victories.

And what this building meant to Snooks Kelley. It was the object of his greatest pride, and I suppose in a sense this building really meant all the world to him because, in a true sense, it was his world. I visited John just a couple of days ago. He is aware that we are having this celebration tonight. He is certainly with all of us, and is proud of all of the young men whom he had as team members throughout his years as coach. He has been, throughout his illness, surrounded by the memorabilia and the pictures of so many of you who are here. I can certainly assure you that John Kelley will be gratefully remembered in the new building. So throughout all of these marvelous 28 years, McHugh Forum has served Boston College very well. So much of the spirit of Boston College has been formed in this building, through the people who have been its coaches and its players and its athletic directors. And therefore, for all of these 28 years let us be thankful to almighty God, and to each other for our University. And be sure that there is only one reason on earth why we would demolish this building, and that is to replace it with something still better. Thank you all.

CHAPTER II

A PRESIDENT'S PERSPECTIVE ON CHANGE

Introduction

T HE 24 YEARS I had the privilege of serving as president of Boston College constituted almost one-fifth of the University's history. And yet the speed of events and the necessity for constant movement from one engrossing activity to another left little time or inclination for chronicling the change. But dramatic change there was—in student composition and in physical campus, in financial strength and organizational governance, in spirit and aspiration, in faculty colleagueship and productivity, in programmatic diversification and expansion. Arguably, in the last quarter of the 20th century, no other higher educational institution in the country experienced more thoroughgoing and dramatic change than did Boston College.

The following pages will not attempt to write the history of that quarter century. One of my philosophy professors at Louvain used to sketch out the "*grandes lignes*" of a period rather than attempt a running chronology of individual thinkers and their interconnections. The following selections, then, will provide a set of perspectives on the period of my presidency itself rather than upon its individual features.

The Concept of a Religiously Affiliated University

May 20, 1984

Rather than be incompatible with or an adversary to faith, therefore, the university and its questioning are an indispensable counterpart in the effort to keep Christian faith commensurate with the age and ages of mankind.

T HE MOODS OF this beautiful campus over the course of a year run the full spectrum of human feeling—from the wide-eyed expectation of a freshman on his first day away from home—to the exuberance of a victory over Texas—to the unique warmth of Christmas—to nostalgic days of senior week. Yet there is no evening in the course of a year that I look forward to with higher anticipation than Commencement eve—and its gathering of our Fides members.

In a true sense, this group is a tribute to all that is constant and enduring about Boston College; but you also symbolize—as no other group—the rising winds of change that have been carrying Boston College forward. I am not referring to the personal gifts that this small group of individuals has contributed to the college over recent years. I am referring more to the confidence in the University, the enthusiastic belief in what it is about, that can create progress just as effectively as it reflects it.

And so I have much to thank you for—on behalf of the entire college community—and each year I look forward to this evening in order to speak those thanks. In a very special way I want to express my gratitude to our chairman of the past three years, Bert Kelley, who has built so dramatically on the foundation laid by those who went before. And, of course, a double measure of thanks is due to Jim Cleary—who was not only founding chairman of this organization in 1972—but has been the moving force within the President's Circle since he established the group several years ago. Needless to say, I am most grateful to welcome Jack McNeice to succeed Bert as chairman for the coming year.

Through its loyalty and generosity, Fides has become symbolic of advancement. Yet, for a college or university, there is no single measure of progress. This college must meet all the financial and managerial standards of any multimillion dollar business enterprise. It must also meet the more elusive but no less exacting standards of the scholarly community and of an intuitively bright and mobile student body. Perhaps most important of all, it must meet standards it has fashioned for itself out of its own store of ideals and experience and understanding of young men and women and of the world they should create.

Thanks in no small part to the people in this room, I believe that Boston College's progress has been more striking in the past two years than at any time I can recall in the decade of the '70s. Yet heady as it is, progress looks backward because it is measured against the past. If I am any judge, something more important than progress has been taking place over these two years. We have been putting in place the conditions for even more substantial steps in the years ahead.

Let me mention just three of those improved conditions. In the month just past, the necessity of choosing our freshman class from among the 14,300 applicants placed Boston College, for the first time, among the most selective and competitive colleges in the country. In terms of academic resources, the completion of our magnificent new research library and computing center, and the renovation of Bapst Library, will create both the incentive and the means for a type of academic life that has been an undue struggle for several decades. Finally, if talent and resources are twin engines for forward movement, the final ingredient is the subtler quality of enthusiasm and zest. Some people need to look through others' eyes in order to get perspective on themselves. The response that Boston College's growing stature has evoked across the country and from dramatically growing numbers of friends like yourselves, has given the University a sense of confidence that holds promise for every facet of the University's operations.

Patterns of growth and progress are as different for institutions as they are for individual people. If I were asked to locate Boston College along the continuum of growth, despite its venerable 120 years, I would place the college only at the point of young adulthood—indeed, not unlike the situation of our most talented graduates of the morrow. Both we and they are fully aware of recent change that has taken place. Yet, both of us are perhaps just at the point of fully gathering confidence in our own powers and of putting final touches to the high talents that have already been tested, but whose greatest accomplishments lie ahead.

In past years, I have taken the opportunity of our Fides gathering to reflect, however briefly, on one or another distinctive characteristic of the college. In a sense there could be no clearer commentary on the University than the persons of those who will receive honorary degrees tomorrow. In their careers and in their eloquent statements, we can see lived the University's high aspirations for new knowledge and for adapting that knowledge to shape a modern world and to bring its benefits, with compassion, to the neediest people in society. I would like to reflect for just a few moments on the religious character of Boston College that continues to shape its own individual personality as a Catholic university.

For if it is easy enough for us to understand how knowledge

relates to the building of a national economy and its importance to social improvement in society, people can be legitimately puzzled about the connections between faith and the human sciences, between learning and religious experience. The puzzlement is important. Through the knowledge it creates and the technology it makes possible, the university is in large measure the creator of culture. If the notion of a Catholic or a Methodist or Presbyterian university made no sense, if religious beliefs and values were irrelevant or incompatible to the work of the university, those beliefs and values would soon become irrelevant to the world of business and law and the arts. They would soon become irrelevant or incompatible with culture itself.

Certainly, the concept of a religiously affiliated university has a venerable history. In our own country, that concept once breathed life into Princeton and Columbia, into Syracuse and Tufts, into Dartmouth and Yale. But in the last 25 years, institutions of learning and religious bodies have increasingly gone their separate ways, convinced perhaps that each would be more free to be themselves by living apart. Obviously, any complete understanding of the evolution of American universities and religious faiths in recent years would require patient historical analysis and not a little philosophizing that are too recondite for this setting.

But whatever the historical circumstances of any individual university's separation from its religious aspirations, the fact of the matter is that the concept of a religiously affiliated university is a difficult one. It attempts to combine into a single entity two of the most powerful and original forces in world culture; namely, religious faith that responds to God's communication of truth in history and the controlled and methodic disciplines of the sciences for understanding the intricacies of the surrounding world. In their origins these two forces do not rely upon each other. They stand separate, autonomous; and in their individual worth, they merit a freedom to pursue their own paths and to be answerable to their own authority. Because they are so radically different, therefore, the powers of religious faith and the power of human understanding carry seeds of inner tension—some would say the earmarks of total incompatibility.

And yet the puzzlement extends even further.

One of religious faith's fundamental beliefs to a man or a woman is its calm assurance, not of an individual's final lot, but of the ultimate origin and meaning of human existence. On the other hand, the precise creating of the intellectual disciplines lies in their urgency to question and inquire and to cross old frontiers. Without attempting to extend the analysis of the prerogatives of faith and religion, or of inquiry and science and university, it should already be clear that any combining of these two sets of forces will be difficult. And yet, if one were to become irrelevant or adversary to the other, both would suffer irreparably as would the society that depends upon them.

Esoteric as this puzzle may appear, of how to relate faith and science, assurance and questioning, commitment and freedom, it is perhaps this audience that is ideally situated to understand the connection.

The French philosopher, Gabriel Marcel, likens religious faith to the unconditional, perduring love of one person to another. Marcel compares faith to human love because of two of love's characteristics. It can be spoken once and for all in a single word, and yet be clarified and deepened and expanded throughout a lifetime. It can be irrevocably given once, yet renewed and give new life through a history. Love attempts to speak a last word yet it always remains a promise open to a future. The conditions for love's growth are many. It grows in those questionings that accompany the birth of children, the making of new friends, the evolution of the family's social and economic life. It grows too in those situations where new questions are addressed by spouses to each other—not in a spirit of doubting love once given, but with an honest concern for light not seen, for an illumination equal to a new situation. In short, love remains constant without losing its mobility; it does not cease to be a light even while asking new questions that are part of life itself.

This same resilience and mobility and capacity for growth is the mark of a living faith. Faith grows and develops not only in isolation, but in those healthy questionings and involvements of a sincere engagement with science and industry and the arts that are creators of culture. Faith is always, at best, a dark light. Changed social and cultural and historical situations prompt questions not in any spirit of unfaith or of retracting a trust once given, but with a genuine concern for light not seen, for an illumination equal to a new situation. Rather than be incompatible with or an adversary to faith, therefore, the university and its questioning are an indispensable counterpart in the effort to keep Christian faith commensurate with the age and ages of mankind.

The point is that in the familiar living of human love there is room for sincere questioning, which neither suspends nor abdicates love once given, nor descends to the level of play-acting, where all the answers are known before the questions are asked. And within the serious business of living within the dark circle of faith, there is room for those sincere questions that arise from an evolving science or culture or philosophy that are neither abdications of faith nor insincere role-playing.

There is a second and final characteristic of human love between persons that can provide the formula for combining the disparate elements within the religiously affiliated university. The relationship of human love, for all of its perfection, is never fixed or finished, or static or immobile. It is always susceptible to growth and, therefore, it is always fragile and leaves each person perpetually vulnerable. For that very reason, human love calls upon the very best in both parties—the recognition that neither is self-sufficient, but paradoxically each depends upon the other if they are to be fully themselves. This implies not a little humility, on the part of each, and much respect directed to the other. As all of you know, therefore, human love is no simple phenomenon. It calls for mutual respect and the willingness to receive as well as to give. It calls for courage as much as for tolerance. And it calls for the willing acceptance of risk without which nothing can be gained through growth because nothing can be lost.

In the course of religiously affiliated universities, these characteristics of love have not always been observed. Whenever either party, be it religious faith or the power of human sciences, lost courage or lost humility or lost the ability to respect and receive from the other, the vulnerable link dissolved. But for all its vulnerability, I am sure that you recognize that human love still constitutes the leaven that makes all human growth possible. And in a true sense, a firm link between the religious beliefs and aspirations of a society and its university settings is a critical ingredient for the growth of culture. That link is as fragile and yet enriching as the link of love itself.

In the loyalty and dedication of members of Fides to Boston College, you make possible not only our contributions of knowledge to society and its application to a developing culture; you also make possible our living out the fragile and humble, but critically important, task of maintaining religious belief and the human arts and sciences together in their productive union.

And for this we thank you most of all.

The One Millionth Volume
for the Boston College Libraries
September 22, 1987

*If librarians are known for their scholarly competence and
their judgment, I have come to look upon them as
truly passionate people who have a zeal and an unrelenting
urgency for accumulating intellectual resources
that shape the individual character of
all great libraries.*

ONE COULD READ the invitation to today's ceremony
and regard it as a totally prosaic, indeed impersonal event.
On the surface, we celebrate two lifeless entities: a book and
a number.

But if the brevity of language appropriate to an invitation
had to be confined to the notation of our millionth volume,
all of us who are assembled realize that we are celebrating today a cherished band of individual persons, celebrating their
lofty and urgent ideals that brought the Boston College libraries to this landmark expression of its intellectual wealth.

It is especially appropriate that our newest, most precious
volume is located here in the Burns Library of Rare Books and
Special Collections, that is the home of the University's oldest,
and indeed first, volumes. And what a beautifully appropriate
irony that the generous anonymous benefactor who contributes our newest volume chose not a work on the most modern
technological advances, but a book that takes us back to the
very origins of printing, and that is a striking example of the

way in which people of genuine learning expressed their awe for knowledge by enhancing the written word through the visual arts.

As president of Boston College, I would like to pay simple tribute today to two groups of people, and to their lofty idealism. The architects and builders, and indeed University officials, who have erected this glorious building, have been recognized on occasions past. Today, I would like to express gratitude to the train of learned and judicious and dedicated librarians who, over the past 125 years, have been responsible for the gradual and painstaking growth of our collections to their present impressive state. If librarians are known for their scholarly competence and their judgment, I have come to look upon them as truly passionate people who have a zeal and an unrelenting urgency for accumulating intellectual resources that shape the individual character of all great libraries. Today, we celebrate the passionate ideals of a Tom O'Connell, and a Brendan and Terence Connolly, and Helen Landreth and Jeanne Aber—and of each of the University's librarians whose professionalism and passionate love of learning brought us to this day.

If we justly honor our librarians, we celebrate all of those generations of benefactors whose generosity has made possible the accession of a million volumes into our libraries. As Fr. Joseph Shaw's bequest of his books formed the basis of all our collections, Judge John J. Burns was the first patron of our Library of Rare Books in which the newest volume will reside. I express special gratitude to the Burns family, whose devotion to their father, John J. Burns, and to his loves and ideals, made possible this glorious re-creation of a Gothic home for our special collections.

The Campaign for Boston College

October 14, 1988

Anyone who knows the history of Boston College
knows that it is a history woven not out of wealth
and abundant financial means, but woven out of vision
and courage and out of admiration for things of the mind.

LAST WEDNESDAY NIGHT, for only the second time
in the 125-year history of Boston College, a General of the
Jesuit Order came to campus. In his person, I am sure that
he evoked for his listeners ideals that were at the cornerstone
of Boston College's founding. The centerpiece of his message
was drawn from Boston College itself—that is, from the unusual motto that Boston College selected from the sixth book
of Homer's *Iliad*, where Glaucos describes the inspiration and
challenge that he received from his father as he sailed off with
the Greek Army to distant Troy:

> "Hippolochos, my father, sent me here to Troy
> with solemn charge:
> Ever to excel, to do better than others, and to
> bring glory to your forebears, who were indeed very
> great. This is my ancestry: this is the blood I am
> proud to inherit."

As we gather here this evening in this glistening new building only a stone's throw from the original Boston College,
vestiges of our forebears are all about us, and we ourselves
are testimony that they were indeed, very great. Who can

view the images of our past, sketched on our table programs, and not realize that we are tonight a generation born of generations of vision and courage—and of intense dedication to the mission of Boston College. If there was sacrifice among those generations—and there was courageous sacrifice on the part of families and countless friends—the sacrifice was as nothing because of the value of what they were building. And who can view the colorful images of Boston College's present and fail to realize that our anniversary is a celebration of promise?

This 125th anniversary year has been an occasion for the entire University community to rediscover our continuity with generations past, and to glimpse the promise that recent changes have made possible.

One hundred and twenty-fifth anniversaries do not punctuate the age of institutions with the same power of a centennial celebration. And yet, in our case, I firmly believe that our gathering tonight, both in symbol and in fact, marks Boston College's entrance into a genuinely new era in its life.

Sixteen years ago, Boston College, with countless other colleges and universities in the nation, was emerging from a deep institutional crisis—perhaps the greatest that has challenged American higher education in its history. Financially, the meager resources of the University had dwindled to the point where any further erosion would have been disastrous. Academically, our once majestic buildings were feeling the effects of limited financial means, and a talented student body was frankly confused about the merits of academic pursuits when so many of society's wounds seemed to call for their immediate attention. Unfortunately, too many felt obliged to choose between serious academic work and service to society. The divisions that had rent much of the American populace over war and peace and race and freedom and authority and renewal in the Church had badly frayed, and in some places had broken, the fabric of trust so critical to the learning process and to the colleagueship that is the distinctive strength of a university.

Thankfully, the crisis passed.

During the past 16 years, the same strategies that made the crisis pass helped build the University to its present robust health. Fiscal discipline consistently applied not only averted further financial peril; it made available the resources to restore pride in our handsome campus and make it the educative experience its builders intended. The return of peace and civility in the land and the conscious directing of student and faculty attention to the merits of intellectual pursuits dissolved the necessity of choosing between learning and service. Indeed, both faculty and students, motivated to help others, saw authentic learning once again not as the competitor but at the indispensable condition to improving our world. And as the spirit and pride in Boston College that had been tested but not broken by crisis, reasserted itself, the attractiveness of the College spread from state to state; and while 18-year-olds declined by nearly one-half, students seeking entry to Boston College almost tripled. While uncertain enrollments in other institutions made them less confident to appoint new faculty, Boston College vigorously enriched its ranks. The strategy was systematically to strengthen both faculty standards and compensation, not only to provide the most enriching educational experience to our students, but in order to make Boston College a campus where fundamental advances are made in each of our intellectual disciplines. At the graduate level, last year our law school faculty ranked 13th in scholarly research productivity among all law schools in the nation. Thus far in the decade of the '80s alone, our faculty have published more than 1,800 scholarly books and articles.

There is no unmistakable marker to determine at what precise point an institution as complex as Boston College enters a new phase of its life—any more than there is a clear line defining the difference between youth and adulthood for a young man or woman. During the extensive planning that the College undertook in the process of establishing our goals for the '90s, the evaluations we conducted on each of our academic programs led to the repeated prediction that Boston College was at the threshold of a new phase in its history. By the conclusion of the planning process, we were convinced that transitions into new phases are gradual, evolutionary events, and that in our case, at some indefinable point over the last decade and a half, a threshold had been reached. From my perspective, there are two reasons for declaring we cross that threshold into a new era—tonight.

The dramatic changes that have taken place at Boston College over the past decade, in reinforcing the contributions of our faculty and encouraging research, in rebuilding our libraries and strengthening our academic programs, in enhancing vitality of campus life outside the classroom, were largely accomplished through careful fiscal control, through eminently prudent borrowing, and through tuition advances that, although somewhat drastic, never went beyond those of institutions of comparable quality. As Boston College's operating budget rose, less than 10 percent of our operating revenues in any fiscal year were derived from private gifts and from income on endowment. That proportion must change. This night marks a new era because, for the first time, our trustees have formulated a campaign goal that will make possible an indispensable shift in the way the college finances its faculty and student endeavors.

My second reason for declaring tonight the promise of a new era for Boston College is perhaps more philosophical. Anyone who knows the history of Boston College knows that it is a history woven not out of wealth and abundant financial means, but woven out of vision and courage and out of admiration for things of the mind—not just for the beauty and expressiveness of art and literature and for the job of understanding ourselves and the world we live in, but even more, because of the power genuine understanding brings to the creation of our human cities and their economies and, indeed, to the creation of the city of God among us.

There are many urgent causes deserving of philanthropic support in today's society—to stop drugs, to wipe out homelessness, to eradicate poverty. The thrust of a university is different. Those who have stood with Boston College since its founding, and you who stand with her today, do so because Boston College exists to do the work of the mind that helps build a society, that enriches human life. You who stand with Boston College are builders as well. And through its graduates, for the past 125 years, what a success story of building Boston College has written: Young talents, schooled by dedicated and brilliant teachers, have become cardinals, bishops, judges, physicians, educators, nurses, businessmen and women, writers, legislators, architects, mothers and fathers—and countless men and women who never attracted or desired fleeting notoriety, but whose own lives and families and friendships have been richer in indescribable ways because of Boston College.

But we have grown to a maturity where Boston College now has a responsibility to be a builder of society in a new way, a responsibility to make a more direct contribution to society than through our graduates. We would not be faithful to our own ideals as a Jesuit university if we were content merely to assimilate and conserve and hand on even the very best of yesterday's and today's constantly advancing knowledge. Scholarship preoccupied only with assimilating and conserving even the best of the past, leaves the future to others. To look beyond the limits of what we presently know in order to create new knowledge, calls for judgment and humility as much as it requires creative vision and courage. But through its faculty, Boston College must increasingly be at the forefront of investigation that creates new knowledge, that uses new knowledge in each of our intellectual disciplines to see more deeply still into the meaning of our faith, and of human existence.

A man who builds skyscrapers accepts risk. He tests to their very limits the capabilities of his knowledge and skills. But in the process, he does more than shape the skyline of his city. What he learns becomes the legacy he contributes to everyone who comes after him.

In February of 1908, an alumnus, Dr. John F. O'Brien, chaired a meeting of graduates who, in a single evening, pledged $137,000 to begin construction of the tower building that has become the architectural signature of Boston College. In the 80 intervening years, graduates have placed that signature on every page of the professions, on every page of business and public life, and in the personal story of more than 100,000 graduates. The ground beneath the tower is more firm today. It is circled by students from every state and every corner of the world. The power of a small faculty in a concentrated curriculum has expanded into a program to sharpen every shade of intellectual interest. But Fr. Gasson's tower stands taller tonight because Boston College has fully assumed its university responsibilities, not merely to serve the world by communicating light to its students, but by using its unique talent to create light that will further brighten our world. It is the new height of that tower that makes our campaign necessary and attractive.

I feel the same sense of gratitude tonight that Fr. Bapst felt in 1863 and Fr. Gasson experienced in 1908. I can frankly say that 16 years ago, I could never have envisioned the generosity of so many trustees and graduates and friends who have brought us to the striking goal that we have already achieved.

Without the generosity of Dr. O'Brien and the group he assembled in 1908, Gasson Tower would not have risen, and countless pages in the history of families, of the Church and the nation would have remained blank, or been written in less glowing colors. Eighty years later, on our 125th anniversary, we gather from generation to generation in a celebration of promise.

Because of Jim Cleary and Jack Connors and the generosity of each of you in this room and beyond, the generosity that in the case of the Carroll family spreads across generations, the promise of Boston College's new era will be fulfilled.

Boston College Hosts the Military Order of Malta

September 21, 2001

*I believe it is important that there be at least
some universities that bring religious faith and its values into
dialogue with the other formative disciplines
that influence culture, and do so at the highest level of
professionalism and sophistication.*

K NIGHTS AND DAMES of the Order of Malta:

This is indeed an historic evening. It is a great pleasure for me to be able to welcome all of you to Boston College, for the first time, for your annual Malta Leadership Conference. For more somber reasons, this has been an historic week in the life of our country. I congratulate you for being with us this evening, and I applaud your courage and your initiative as we breathe new spirit into our saddened world. Indeed, it is because of what the nation has suffered that your presence is all the more important. As knights and dames of Malta, you exemplify the very qualities our nation will need in abundance in the years ahead: high talent and human accomplishment enriched and undertaken with deep religious motivation. It is because Boston College shares that same inspiration toward high human accomplishment infused with deep religious motivation, that we are so pleased to welcome you this evening.

Clearly, the architecture and the décor of our setting this evening at our downtown club does not reflect the warmth of our collegiate Gothic campus, but I know you will have the opportunity to explore the campus and to hear from several Jesuit members of our faculty tomorrow and Sunday.

This evening, I have been asked to share a view of the University that gets behind some of the day-to-day interaction of faculty and students, between researchers and administrative officers. I would like to attempt, however briefly, to describe where the University has been in recent years, to express some of our current aspirations, and to share with you why we believe that Boston College has a special importance not only to our own graduates, but to the Church and American society.

Through the first 125 years of its history, Boston College had a clear and remarkably consistent portrait. Founded primarily to educate sons of Irish immigrants who had come to the city in vast numbers in the 1840s and '50s, the College from the beginning had a demanding curriculum that required its admission policies to be selective. From 1863 to the mid-20th century, the College focused on quality undergraduate education, and through the first half of the 20th century, on selective graduate and professional schools. Its focus was quality teaching and student learning, rather than on basic or applied research. On its hundredth anniversary in 1963, the then-president, Fr. Michael Walsh, deliberately set the institution on an explicitly university course, that is, to add and heighten the emphasis upon graduate and doctoral programs in all schools of the University with the obvious prerequisite of focusing not only on the transmission of knowledge, but upon the creation of new knowledge through basic and applied research.

Unfortunately, the crisis that engulfed all of higher education from 1968 to 1972 all but extinguished the high aspirations that the College was successfully pursuing in the early '60s. During those four short years, students were almost immobilized by the seeming dilemma between the subtle claims of academic study and the urgency of direct social action to cure the nation's wounds of race and of poverty and of Vietnam. These social crises that swept through every campus were heightened at Boston College by the dramatic changes that came about in Catholic life in the wake of the Second Vatican Council. Centuries-old signposts of Catholicity, from meatless Fridays and Latin liturgies to the Church's loosening of its reliance on scholastic methodologies in philosophy and theology, left too many, both alumni and University staff, uncertain as to what was the authentically Catholic and what its betrayal. The stress arising from these profound social conflicts struck at exactly the time when the managerial capabilities of the University were already struggling to increase the professionalism and discipline that the complexity of a modern university required.

In 1972, the student body, drawn from an annual 6,000 applicants principally from the Northeast region, remained strong. But in the words of one of our most experienced trustees, Boston College in 1972 was unbankable. Its net worth was negative, all reserves were exhausted, its $4 million endowment was so restricted as to be operationally useless; the University's Catholic character was being questioned, its academic priorities weakened, its sense of community driven by suspicion and distrust born of ideological differences.

If the University's problems were deep and therefore serious, they at least had the advantage of being clear and of presenting a logical coherence so that they could be addressed in order. Obviously, the most pressing problem was financial. If no way of resolving it could be found, there would be no need to address the others.

I am obviously not going to attempt to detail the managerial steps employed in changing each of these impending dangers into a new source of initiative. However, with the encouragement of our Board of Trustees, strategic planning of one sector of the University after another was one of our key tools, and the process of planning itself gradually turned suspicion and distrust into mutual respect and wholehearted cooperation. In a word, those strategic efforts successively produced: a financial plan that began a string of 30 straight balanced budgets; successive academic plans that redefined academic goals at the center of our priorities; capital plans that led to the addition of 36 major new or totally refurbished buildings; not only new definition of our Catholic and Jesuit character, but the creation of our Jesuit Institute and Center for Jesuit Spirituality as means to assure its continued vitality.

The end result is that, for the past decade, Boston College has found itself at the undergraduate level among the top 40 institutions in the country, and all but one of its graduate schools ranked among the top 25, with the only outlier among the top 40. Our once meager endowment this year stands at $1.1 billion, half of it unrestricted. Our first-year undergraduates are among the most selective student bodies in the country, chosen from 20,000 aspirants from all 50 states and scores of foreign countries. In a world that has seen increasing stratification of colleges and universities on the basis of quality, Boston College today finds itself on an altogether new plateau, increasingly at the top stratum of the best universities in the land.

All of this, of course, is well and good. But I have gone through this admittedly long story of dramatic change with you not to display some narrow form of elitism. Indeed, there are those who occasionally look wistfully back to our days as only Boston's College and worry that in diversifying our clientele we have diluted our mission. I have gone into this changing history because I believe that as knights and ladies of Malta, you are in a position to recognize why we believe that Boston College's degree of academic quality and its standing on the same plateau of the best 40 of its national peers is not only important to our local community; that quality and standing have new importance for the Church and have importance to our society.

It has become a truism for all of us that as we cross into the 21st century, we exist not only in an information age where technologies have allowed us to create and manage and almost drown ourselves in increasing access to information; it is perhaps even more an intellectual age where the formative elements of the cultures which surround us are shaped not by our natural environment and its forces, but by human imagination and intelligence. They are shaped by our technologies, our business policies and practices, by our hard science, shaped not only by our increasingly versatile communications media, but by the literary and artistic and dramatic sensibilities they encourage. Our culture shapes and is shaped by our economic theories and the forces they engender. It is shaped by the aesthetic and ethical and religious values that it espouses or fails to espouse.

Today, all sorts of corporations and think tanks and public relations firms have, through their research, become part of this knowledge industry, but the intellectual disciplines and the research that advances them will always be the primary objective of the world's universities. It is for that reason that universities have had such a powerful influence in the development of Western culture.

Unfortunately, at the very time when the problems facing developed cultures, and the problems separating developing and developed cultures, are less and less technological and more and more valuational, too much of the university world, both public and private, has cut any institutional relationship to religious faith and the religious values that have been so formative an element in human cultures.

No single university has a corner on the myriad intellectual forces that shape a culture. But at the university level where knowledge is not just being transmitted, but is being created, at the university level where research unveils not only what technology and economic policy can do, but confronts questions of what technology and public policy should do, I believe it is important that there be at least some universities that bring religious faith and its values into dialogue with the other formative disciplines that influence culture, and do so at the highest level of professionalism and sophistication. I believe there should be at least some universities that, like you in your personal lives, have the talent and the capabilities for the highest accomplishment, but pursue that accomplishment with a worldview and a set of values that are derived from faith.

The number of Catholic universities in America that achieve that level of accomplishment is small; retaining that level in a continually improving field will be difficult. But that precisely is our aspiration and the source of our special contribution to the Church and American society. Of one thing I am sure: there is no substitute for quality, no substitute for excellence, either in the Church or in academic life. That form of excellence we are pursuing.

The Inspiration of Bernini's Columns and Gasson Tower

May 21, 1989

*Commencement ceremonies dramatize the nature of
the university itself.*

Four years ago, I took the theme of my pre-Commencement dinner remarks from the lyrics of "the loveliest night of the year." I meant to emphasize, of course, the beauty of our surroundings, and especially the joyfulness of the occasion we celebrate. And yet to single out one evening as loveliest is, I suppose, to imply a workaday, uneventful character to most other days in the academic calendar.

Tonight the beauty and the joyfulness are all about us in measures as abundant as any year previously. And yet this year Commencement eve does not stand out in contrast to the background of the months just past. It seems rather to be a final and joyful salute to an entire academic year that has been marked by splendid accomplishments.

There are usually cycles to our seasons—from winter to spring, from darkness to light—but every now and then we are blessed with a succession of cloudless days that suffer no interruption.

The academic year just closing was, from September to May, just such a year.

Many of you were participants in the events that looked backward in celebration of anniversaries reached and at others placing foundations upon which this University will build into the next century.

Sincere gratitude and a measure of justified pride were the constant themes as the University this fall celebrated its 125th anniversary—and welcomed for only the second time in our history, the superior general of the Jesuit order to lead both student and alumni gatherings in expression of thanksgiving. In certainly the largest airlift from Boston since World War II, thousands of graduates joined our athletic teams in revisiting the land of immigrant children Boston College was originally founded to educate. In fall and winter, two handsome residences opened their doors as further testaments to the national reach of our student body, 96 percent of whom now request resident rather than commuting status at the college. Our Wallace E. Carroll School of management celebrated its 50th anniversary by assuming into its own title the name of an alumnus whose singular generosity has provided leadership for each of the University's initiatives over the past 30 years. With the name of one great Boston college alumnus and House Speaker already gracing our new state-of-the-art library system, this year also witnessed ceremonies in which one of his congressional associates and three other Boston College graduates gave their names to the athletic facility they were so instrumental in making possible.

In October in Boston, and in April in New York, the University commemorated its 125th anniversary by looking forward, to establish a campaign fund that will preserve and enhance the quality of the University in years ahead; an extraordinary testimony to the esteem and sacrifice the University has inspired through its accomplishments. Only three weeks ago, the College hosted the first national conference of our Jesuit Institute to open a new chapter in the intellectual contributions this University will make as American culture continues to seek new vitality from its political and literary and religious roots.

Commencement weekend, however, is not just one more ceremonial event in the institutional life of a university. Dedicating a building, or inaugurating a conference series, or competing for a national championship—each makes its impact on the University—but the Commencement ceremonies dramatize the nature of the university itself.

Three weeks ago I had the privilege of spending 10 days in Rome as one of 18 American College presidents to participate with colleagues from 40 nations around the world who were invited to provide advice to the Vatican congregation on higher education. An outline of the results of the gathering has appeared in many organs of the public press and I shall not expand upon that outline here. The meeting, however, was remarkably successful in taking full advantage of the breadth of experience of the participants. Through patient discussion, we were able to achieve almost unanimous consensus on 10 foundational principles we considered important for any eventual statement on Catholic higher education. But I recall the meeting this evening not to comment upon its process or to enumerate the principles arrived at, but because the complete setting of the meeting and its topic of the Catholic university in a sense expand the meaning of our gathering this evening.

What is there about this 11th-century invention of the university that still merits assembling hundreds of university officials and churchmen from every continent to discuss its nature? And if it continues to be important in a world revolutionized by technology and divided by language and legal system and degree of economic development, what are the conditions under which the university can continue to exercise its beneficial influence?

Our delegates met in small paneled conference rooms of 30 and in plenary auditorium sessions of 200. Our languages differed. Catholic universities in Korea and Tokyo spoke of student bodies 10 percent of which are Christian. In a country, by contrast, with an overwhelmingly Catholic population, such as Poland, government restrictions until now have made any full-scale Catholic university impossible. Universities in Chile reflect the precariously controlled political situation of that country. And for all the newly developing countries of the Southern Hemisphere, the university stands as a tall but ever so slender beacon to light the advance of whole populations.

But however different our languages or our national background, there was a unanimous, powerful conviction abroad that on the world scene the university, and the Catholic university, has entered a new era. Cultural advances in our lifetime have simultaneously made the university's responsibilities greater, its standards of effectiveness more exacting.

In a simpler, less sophisticated world, simpler forces shaped our culture—the family, the parish, the radio, or monthly movie—indeed, the liberal education of an undergraduate college.

For better or worse, today's cultures are shaped by more sophisticated forces. The growing knowledge explosion and the communication and technological revolutions that have taken place since World War II have made the university not less, but dramatically more important in shaping the direction of human culture.

I perhaps never saw more clearly than through the eyes of a president from Bombay and one from Brazil and another from Zaire that the university's research and training and its standards of values that are larger than those of business and government are indispensable channels along which a nation's culture takes shape and communicates its benefits to a larger population.

Indeed, so influential has the university become in today's society that if the Church's belief and its values are to play a formative role in tomorrow's culture, they must do so through their presence in the world of the Catholic university.

But if the university stands taller in today's society, the tests of its quality have never been more exacting. Yesterday's methods and organizational structures, in business or in government, will not confer tomorrow's leadership. Nor will they do so in university life. Standards of professionalism in scholarship, in the management of persons and resources, in the artfulness needed to reach new clienteles call for a range of talents and of resources as broad as society itself. In one sense, the thrust of our entire meeting in Rome was to summarize and project ahead the manner in which Catholic universities the world over are meeting their new responsibilities for professionalism while still assuring that the religious beliefs and values that have been formative in shaping past cultures will exercise their influence in the cultures we continue to create.

Our conversations from 40 different countries made clear that there is no single model or formula to eliminate the tensions between the thoroughgoing professionalism of today's university and keeping meaningful its religious inspiration—any more than there is a single model or formula to balance consuming responsibilities to one's business and to one's family. Where we were unanimous, however, was in affirming the imperative urgency of maintaining both. Professionally inadequate Catholic universities will not serve the needs of today's society. A Catholic university devoid of Christian inspiration will serve neither its faith nor the national purpose that encourages independent institutions precisely in order to blend into its own life the accent of religious traditions.

If eight days of discussion produced no formula for the Catholic university to meet the exacting demands of its new responsibilities, it did provide scores of examples of its accomplishment. Indeed, it was not in our discussions in modern conference rooms, but rather among the silent monuments of ancient Rome that I recognized older, perhaps more striking examples, of the blend of religious inspiration with the most ambitious ideals of human accomplishment. For alongside Christianity's belief in its divine origin, it has had perhaps no rival in the confidence and support and encouragement it has given to the full blossoming of human talent in the form of the arts and architecture, in scholarship and medical science. As the light faded from St. Peter's square one of those evenings, I strolled through those vast spaces and marveled at the sweep of columns and the architectural forms against the sky. There stood the tangible, breathtaking expression from another age of Christian inspiration operating through the most exacting disciplines of human art and architecture—indeed, bringing those arts to a new perfection for their time. That tradition is the challenging one in which to stand.

In large measure thanks to you, Boston College's place in that tradition is today a lofty one. For in the precise years when the managerial and technical and financial demands of professionalism became urgent, more and more of you stepped forward as never before to make your judgment, your expertise, and your financial means a part of this University.

Indeed, with your presence on such a night as this, would it be presumptuous for me to speak the name of Bernini's majestic columns and of our stately towers in the same breath?

24 Years as 18 Holes of Golf: Brae Burn Country Club

October 6, 2000

When it comes time to hand in a scorecard, sometimes even the players are pleasantly surprised.

I N T H E M O R E than 20 years that I have been a member of Brae Burn, this is the first time I have been obliged to sing for my supper. When Royce Taylor asks, however, how can one refuse? Royce was one of the visiting team who came to evaluate my social skills as a potential member of Brae Burn years ago, and as I looked through my Brae Burn file in preparation for this evening, I found early communications with Norman MacNeil, who was president of the club at that time, and, of course, with Dick Crosby, who could not have been more welcoming to me in the club and especially on the course. Though they regrettably are no longer with us, each of them communicated a sense of refinement and a genuine love of golf that make the club what it is to all of us today.

When Royce approached me about speaking to you, he suggested that perhaps I could weave together, in some way, the game of golf and what I have been doing with the rest of my life over the past 20 years.

As most of you already know, I served as president of Boston College for the 24 years from 1972 to 1996. Prior to that, I had served as a dean and, perhaps more interestingly, was a professor of ethics at the college level for 10 years. Drawing parallels between the game of golf and university administration, much less with the discipline of ethics, might be a considerable reach. But book after book has been written showing that sports are a metaphor for life, so here goes!

There was at least one perfect parallel in my attitude toward golf and toward the possibility of one day being a university president. I had decided early on that I wanted nothing to do with either. Early in life, I resolved I would not play golf until I was too old for all the more active sports that I enjoyed. And after a four-year stint as an academic dean, I had concluded that teaching and writing books was much more to my liking than university administration. But at 21, I took my first swing at a golf ball, and have been playing ever since. And when asked to enter the search for the presidency of Boston College in the summer of 1972, the very real attractions of the classroom had to give way to the possibility of a broader type of service to students and to education.

Perhaps the most striking difference from the game of golf is that running a university is always a team sport. Managing a $300 million budget to educate 14,000 students while building and repairing and maintaining a hundred major buildings and keeping the University abreast of an absolute revolution in technology, is not a game you play by yourself, and it is certainly not a game that you win by yourself. Any success that Boston College has had over the past 30 years has been the success of a remarkably talented and dedicated team of administrators and trustees and faculty and staff ... and of a good many friends standing along the fairways who gave an encouraging cheer and, I suspect, occasionally kicked the ball out of the rough when we were in danger of a triple bogey.

At the end of the day, every player turns in a scorecard. But the fun in the game is not just in the numbers on the card; it's in a few memorable shots, and perhaps even more importantly, in your course management for the day—how the winds were blowing and how you understood where the hazards were and what was the slope of the fairways and where the pitch in the greens.

Royce obviously knew that, on the 19th hole, golfers are infinitely patient in listening to each other analyze their afternoon. So at the risk of replaying a game that has long been over, I hope it will be informative for me to recall where the winds were coming from when I arrived on the first tee at Boston College in 1972—what the hazards were and where the fairways sloped away into the rough.

The winds that were blowing in 1972 came from the Vietnam War and the social upheavals of the late 1960s, they came from the Vatican Council that in so many ways changed the face of what it meant to be Catholic, and they came from the individualized growing pains of an institution whose increasing complexity made a new style of professionalized management an absolute condition of survival. And I can tell you frankly that those winds were so strong that they almost blew us off the course on the first three holes that we faced.

I am sure that all of you experienced in your own homes and perhaps among your own families some of the effects of the dramatic social changes that took place between 1968 and 1972. Perhaps no institutions felt those changes more acutely than did America's colleges and universities, which in some ways became the battleground for all the conflicting forces. In the face of the moral dilemmas arising from Vietnam and the deep social upheavals involving race and poverty, students found themselves caught on the horns of a dilemma between the value of academic pursuits and the urgency of direct social action to heal the wounds in American society. So many of them were caught in the urgency of social causes that they lost sight of the value of learning that only a university can provide. When a faculty daily faces students uncertain of the value itself of learning, it is easy to have uncertainty about priorities seep into the institution itself.

Because universities were a battleground, they all too often became the stage for strong hostilities, and if not open hostility, the stage for suspicion and distrust, between young and old, black and white, pro-war and anti-war, students and faculty, faculty and administration.

Every university in the country, Boston College included, felt these winds, tried to negotiate these hazards. The fact that Boston College was a Church-related, Catholic institution exposed it to winds that others did not feel. The Second Vatican Council that came to a close in 1965 radically changed not the substance of the faith of Catholics, but a whole range of practices in how Catholics worshipped (in the liturgy of the Mass changing from Latin to the vernacular), in some long traditional observances such as abstaining from meat on Friday, and perhaps even more importantly for universities, in relaxing its reliance on the scholastic method of doing philosophy and doing theology in favor of more eclectic methodologies. Without belaboring the point, the fact is that through the process of assimilating the changes of Vatican II, there was a period of widespread confusion and misunderstanding and alienation over what it meant to be Catholic. For Boston College, the end result was that too many of its most dedicated graduates and friends began to doubt whether it had lost its sense of intellectual priorities and its identity as Catholic.

But the most immediate hazard facing the College in 1972 came not from Vietnam or from Rome's Vatican II. The most immediate challenge was financial. Over the previous four years in an effort to meet rising deficits, all available reserves were exhausted. Thanks to the understanding and the courage of our banker, Giles Mosher, a substantial credit line allowed us to meet payrolls. But any recurrence of the deficits would have left no option but to pull the credit line and threaten bankruptcy. Fortunately, by the time of my arrival in the summer of 1972, the first steps in meeting the challenge had already been taken.

One of the reasons for recurring operating deficits had been the frightening weakness of financial systems and controls. In 1971, our board appointed a brilliantly creative financial vice president from Raytheon who had begun the process of professionalizing our fiscal operations. But with controls in place, what we needed was a financial plan that would keep revenues and expenditures in balance over a sustained period of time. Any further slippage could have, would have, spelled disaster.

I am obviously not going to try to recount every shot or explain every strategy that we used in negotiating these hazards. One of our primary weapons that never lost its power was a process of strategic planning successively applied to various segments of the University. In 1972, the most immediate need, of course, was for a realistic financial plan, and in September of that year, we began just such a financial strategic effort that eight months later resulted in a plan that assured us of a future. It would be hard to estimate the height of the boost in morale that took place when the very real cloud of bankruptcy faded from the sky.

But the process of planning did something more. It proved to be a powerful form of trust-building between faculty and administrative officers, an experience of colleagueship that overcame suspicions that had wasted physical and psychic energies in opposing one another, rather than cooperatively working in concert.

On the basis of success in setting a realistic financial framework in place, we were able to turn the same, simple tool of strategic planning to reestablish our academic priorities as a university, and a realistic sense of what it means to be a Catholic university.

Strategic planning, then, was a managerial tool we employed over and over again to provide a clear framework for all we did. In the middle of a golf game, it is easy to let one good hole, or one bad hole, make you lose sight of the big picture—the entire 18. Maintaining a 10-year plan that we rolled forward every year always kept our eye on the big picture as we negotiated the ups and downs of everyday play.

Obviously, a good game plan, by itself, doesn't win ball games, or golf games—or success as a university. It takes good players, with good skills, some great shot-making; and there's no doubt but that sunny weather and well-kept fairways and neat greens contribute to the score.

As I mentioned earlier, we were fortunate in assembling a first-class team of vice presidents and deans and middle managers and faculty—some of whom came up with brilliant shots when they were most needed. And gradually, as though after a few tough holes, the memory of Vietnam and near bankruptcy did fade, and clouds of mistrust did dissolve. The sun came out and the putts began to drop.

When it comes time to hand in a scorecard, sometimes even the players are pleasantly surprised. In our case, the meager $4 million endowment of 1972 today stands at over a billion, one. The quality of our undergraduate students reflects winnowing not a pool of 6,000, but of 21,000 applicants. Each of our grad schools are ranked among the top 50, most in the top 25.

I can honestly say that I've never had a day at Brae Burn that I haven't enjoyed. And I can say the same about every one of the 28 years of days at Boston College.

Perhaps the biggest difference between my visits to Brae Burn these days, and my life at Boston College is this: At this point in life, with the scorecard turned in, I can go out on the course and not worry about playing to the handicap of the past 25 years. Keeping the handicap where it is, is someone else's job. Like Mickey Lane, I can remain available to tell war stories of the good old days.

Lynch School of Education's Golden Anniversary

October 24, 2002

*The decades have brought a heightened awareness that
the religious dimension of our educational mission, just as much
as in decades past, provides the University with a unique
vantage point to make its contribution within the front ranks of
the American higher educational community.*

I AM VERY HAPPY you are with us to celebrate the 50th anniversary of our Carolyn and Peter Lynch School of Education. I must admit that it came as something of a shock to realize that I had served as president or chancellor of the University for a full 30 of those 50 years. But that lengthy tenure has also given me perspective to realize that at age 50, an individual person or an institution is just coming into the fullness of its mature powers.

When the School of Education was established in 1952, I was just completing the first three years of my teaching experience at St. Peter's College in Jersey City. It was a period when Jesuit colleges throughout the Northeast were experiencing vigorous growth and increased complexity. The expansion into graduate and professional schools was not only a sign of the universities' more direct engagement with the needs of the communities around us; as time went on, it became one of the compelling reasons for increased professionalization of the faculties and of the management of the universities themselves. We have had a full day to recollect some of the most memorable events of these 50 years. From my own vantage point, I have the conviction that none other of our individual schools in the University has enjoyed a faster pace of progress in academic quality than did the School of Education.

In no other of our schools is its reputation for distinction so closely associated with imaginatively creative programs and the individuals responsible for them: Counseling Psychology; the Campus School; high-stakes testing; our PSAP program; teaching internships in countries abroad; our unique form of Upward Bound; our interdepartmental multiservice program in Brighton schools. Against the horizon of strong staple curricula and concentrations, those programs and the names of Fr. Charles Donovan and Sr. Josephina, and John Eichorn and Bill Cottle and Pierre Lambert and John Travers and Mary Kinnane blended easily both temporally and in stature with those of Diana Pullin and Frank Kelly and Mary Griffin and George Madaus and Phil Altbach and Mary Walsh and Joe O'Keefe and Mary Brabeck and John Dacey and George Ladd. And of course, the educational research spearheaded by John Walsh now permeates the entire faculty, and this dimension of their work has become one of the touchstones of the enviable standing the school now enjoys among its peers.

If quantitative measures reflect the Lynch School of Education's stature among its peers, however, the new confidence and institutional power that have developed in dealing with the dramatically changing culture of the past 50 years have significantly deepened the school's own sense of identity and its clarity of mission. Key to that identity is a deliberately chosen sense of colleagueship and community based on sincere respect among all members of the school; a deepened commitment to the worth of scholarship and of learning not just for their own intrinsic value, but for the indispensable light they provide to improve the lives of new generations of students. And enriching that identity is an enlarged sense of justice and of Christian love that perceives the breadth of human need and how the University's resources of mind and heart can address it.

Finally, the decades have brought a heightened awareness that the religious dimension of our educational mission, just as much as in decades past, provides the University with a unique vantage point to make its contribution within the front ranks of the American higher educational community.

My congratulations to each of you—students, graduates, faculty members, deans corps—for the glowing history you have created and are creating for the Lynch School of Education at Boston College. I join you in the certainty that, thanks to you, the past is only prelude to an even brighter future.

A Personal Farewell

May 1, 1996

*A hockey player is only given a few short
minutes of intense activity on the ice and then he yields
his place to a new line and skates to the sideline
to watch the action.*

The following remarks are from a ceremony at the close of my 24 years as president of Boston College. The program included music, messages from trustees, professors, staff, and students, and a video montage of events from those years.

FOR MONTHS I have realized that there was no way to prepare for this day. I could put a few words on paper—but how do you prepare emotionally for the extravaganza we have just witnessed? How do you prepare for the presence of all of you?

When I arrived at Boston College 24 years ago, I chose not to have an inauguration ceremony. I am sure that nothing we could have conjured up for an inaugural in 1972 could have matched the imagination and the sentiment and the sheer fun that every element of today's program has provided.

I am confident you know how grateful I am to each of the persons who orchestrated this program and participated in it—from Geoff Boisi, the chairman of the board, to the newest first-year member of the Chorale and to all of our staff members and faculty in between who reflect the richness of this great University. Among all of you who have come from far and near in such vast numbers I recognize a depth of friendship and of feeling that is truly humbling—but is also the source of my deepest gratitude.

The story of Boston College over the past 24 years that we have just read in our program and heard spoken from this platform and seen unfold on screen is a story of remarkable change. Even if we strip away the aura in which that story was cast this afternoon, the undeniable fact is that the portrait that Boston College projects to the world today is a far different one than the worried profile of 1972. If it is a sign of love to rejoice in the well-being of one we love, then we all certainly rejoice in the blessings of Boston College.

Both in picture and in word those who have preceded me to this platform have more than adequately helped us relive these 24 years. I shall therefore be very brief.

In a spirit of candor I would like to begin with something of a personal confession. When I accepted the invitation from the Board of Trustees in 1972 to serve as president, my familiarity with the University was necessarily limited to a mere outline of academic programs and finances and personnel profiles and student trends. And there was more than enough even in that fulsome outline to make one wary. But I accepted the invitation for two reasons—because, to be sure, there was a clear need; but principally because of an idea—because of my belief in the value and the importance of Jesuit higher education that was my professional and religious vocation, wherever I was to live it.

What changed that dutiful decision into the exhilaratingly happy experience of the past 24 years—was really all of you—and those who had gone before you: faculty and staff and graduates and Jesuits and administrative officers and trustees and parents and students of Boston College. On this striking campus in this privileged city, you had given the idea of Jesuit higher education a compellingly human face and an aspiration for excellence that was to set it forever apart.

The part all of you in this room played in the transformation of Boston College did not take place just once. For 24 unbroken years I have had the continuing realization that whatever responsibility I had for Boston College, it was a responsibility enthusiastically shared by thousands of willing hands—on campus and off, among students and staff, parents and friends, trustees and graduates. It is impossible to pay people to be responsible to an institution. Taking responsibility for an institution is a free gift that springs from love and admiration. And love can never be repaid or compensated. It can only be returned.

That is why I appreciate so much the uniqueness of our gathering today. Indeed, in the past 24 years I cannot recall any assembly that better represented the full spectrum of individuals whose proven friendship and love for Boston College has meant so much to the University and so much to me. Each of your contributions has been different—from the student volunteer leading an enthusiastic tour of campus and the housekeeping crew who stayed on duty 36 hours straight to furnish a new dorm for arriving students, to the trustee who took the red-eye back from California because his voice was needed on an important issue. In so many cases you yourselves did not grasp the full importance to us of what you did. But because each of your contributions was different, they formed a mosaic of strength and of beauty that could have been created in no other way.

And so on this day I could never have foreseen 24 years ago, there is much newfound gratitude but continuing pride in having served as president of Boston College: a pride that is clear-eyed enough to recognize excellence and rejoice in it; but a pride that is astute enough to trace accomplishment to its origins where there stands not one person—but a legion even larger than this room and the love of a provident God whose creative designs we have together been privileged to help fashion.

But best of all, we stand this afternoon not at an end but only at a transition point. Pride and gratitude do not lead to dead ends. The deeper our pride, the more it inspires ambition. The more sincere our gratitude for what we have received from each other, the more we can accomplish.

It is for that reason that I view the transition to the new presidency of Fr. William Leahy three months from today with a sense of increasingly high ambition for Boston College. I realize that the magnitude and the complexity of the responsibilities he will assume are much larger than those that awaited me in 1972. And yet these past 24 years have taught me, if teaching were ever needed, that ambitions for an institution as complex as a modern university do not depend on its president. The talent and dedication and goodwill and generosity of literally thousands of people will play their part in shaping its future. If the challenges of the presidency in 1996 are greater, the prospects of increasing excellence are all the more compelling; the hands to assist in making it a reality are so much more numerous and energetic.

And as for me—a hockey player is only given a few short minutes of intense activity on the ice and then he yields his place to a new line and skates to the sideline to watch the action. The fact that my own turn on the ice has been so long has made it all the more enjoyable. And the best part is that even if I never score another goal, I will continue to be a member of the team and perhaps enjoy the action even more while watching from behind the protective glass.

Blessed Mother Teresa of Calcutta and companion with fellow honoree J. Donald Monan, S.J., and Harvard President Derek Bok (Harvard Commencement, 1982)

President J. Donald Monan, S.J., Prime Minister Garrett FitzGerald, Speaker O'Neill, President Reagan (O'Neill Dinner, Washington, D.C., March 17, 1986)

Board Executive Committee (1993–94). Standing L–R: David S. Nelson, William F. Connell, Edward M. O'Flaherty, S.J., Thomas A. Vanderslice, Judith B. Krauss, John M. Connors, Jr., James F. Cleary. Seated L–R: Vice Chair Richard F. Syron, Father Monan, Chair Geoffrey T. Boisi

Wall Street Council co-founders Geoffrey T. Boisi (second from left) and William J. Vouté (fourth from left) with Father Monan and other Council members

Campaign leaders John M. Connors, Jr. (middle) and James F. Cleary with Father Monan

University vice presidents (September 1989). Standing L–R: Kevin P. Duffy, James P. McIntyre, Margaret A. Dwyer, John R. Smith, John T. Driscoll. Seated L–R: Frank B. Campanella, William B. Neenan, S.J., Paul LeComte

Executive and Financial Vice President John R. Smith (left) and Vice President Frank B. Campanella with Father Monan

Vice President Peg Dwyer with Father Monan

Professor Michael McFarland, S.J., student representative Leondardine Pacombe (CSOM '96), John J. Neuhauser, Geoffrey T. Boisi and J. Donald Monan, S.J. (Fulton Hall reopening, September 19, 1995)

Academic Vice President Charles F. Donovan, S.J., and Brandy

O'Neill Library dedication ceremony (October 14, 1984)

Dedication of renovated Bapst and Burns Libraries (April 22, 1986)

Father Monan, celebrant, with concelebrants William A. Barry, S.J., Robert A. Mitchell, S.J., and priests of the Boston College Community (Mass of the Holy Spirit)

Jesuit faculty Leo O'Keefe (left), Henry Callahan, and William Leonard (right) with Father Monan

Trustee Chair William F. Connell presenting Torch of Leadership Award to J. Donald Monan, S.J. (Boston College Citizen Seminar, 1997)

President's Office receptionist Mary Latson, husband Tim, and daughter Denise

Trustee David S. Nelson with mother, Enid, and Trustee Thomas J. Flatley

Father Monan with Alumni Association Executive Director John Wissler (far left) and his wife Jean, and alumni

Dedication of Conte Forum (1989)

Father Monan with Athletic Director William J. Flynn (August 28, 1990)

Men's hockey coach Len Ceglarski (left), Bill Flynn and Father Monan

Boston College Marching Band

Father Monan with students on the Dust Bowl during the 1970s

Bill Cosby and Father Monan at Commencement (1996)

CHAPTER III

EDUCATION TO REACH
THE HEIGHT AND
BREADTH
OF HUMAN HOPES

Introduction

DOCTORAL STUDENTS COMPOSING dissertations frequently regard university presidents as fertile sources of significant research data. Among the many questionnaires that came across my desk, one that caught my eye inquired into what degree of relevance my own field of doctoral study had to my work as president.

Spontaneously, one might expect that philosophy would have little relevance to the practicalities and managerial responsibilities that fill the ordinary American university president's days. In my own case, however, I had had the good fortune of exploring in my doctoral dissertation the type of judgment or knowing that one employs in decision making—arguably the key responsibility of executive management. Perhaps even more importantly, many of the challenges facing Boston College in the early '70s were ultimately philosophical. To be sure, throughout the decade, in Boston College's case financial pressures were uniquely urgent and an atmosphere of distrust made "hands-on" administration a practical imperative. Nevertheless, deeper philosophic movements were also at work both in the broad spectrum of American higher education as well as throughout the sphere of Catholic colleges and universities.

On the broader front, long-simmering questions about the purpose and primacy of liberal education that had always been the backbone of Boston College's undergraduate education, even in its professional schools, came to the surface. In the Catholic sector, the theological transformation resulting from Vatican II and the urgency of professionalization of university operations raised philosophic questions of Catholic identity that could not be avoided.

Questioning the enterprise of liberal education inevitably opens the door to the most fundamental philosophic questioning of the meaning or the purpose of the human person. What follows in these pages are texts of six speeches, three of which explore a philosophic rationale for the continuing role of liberal education in the development of young men and women. What do institutions of higher learning in America conceive to be the meaning of human life? What do they regard as making life worth living? What is worthy of belief? In a democratic society, I believe that addressing these questions is one of a private college's first obligations and its greatest contribution to the moral tenor of coming decades.

The remaining three speeches in this chapter address a second area of profound philosophic change that took place during the period of my tenure as president of Boston College, namely, the meaning of Catholic identity among American institutions of higher education.

When Pope John Paul II expressed his intention of issuing a modern document on Catholic higher education in the late 1980s, he chose a deliberately consultative process to assist him in its composition. The process continued to be consultative throughout the composition of the Papal Constitution and almost through the completion of its application to the United States nearly 10 years later. First as chairman of the Association of Jesuit Colleges and Universities and for a full decade an appointed member of the Bishops-Presidents Committee, I had the privilege of participating in that consultation.

The consultation began with an invitation for more than a hundred presidents and bishops from around the world to meet in Rome. One purpose of the meetings was to identify, from our experience, characteristics common to the Catholic university. Given the radical diversity of institutions as different as St. Joseph's in Beirut and Sogang University in Korea and Boston College in Massachusetts, it was immediately clear that although each of these were authentically Jesuit universities, in two of them, 90 to 95 percent of their faculty and of their student bodies were not Catholic, were not Christian. What was equally clear, however, was that at the origin of each was an authentically Christian inspiration. The root motivation for the establishment and continuation of each of these institutions lay in the Christian conviction that advancement of learning and of human culture is not only a human good, it plays a contributing role in the development of the Kingdom of God on earth. This conviction, in turn, stems from the uniquely Christian belief that in assuming human nature God gave to our human accomplishments, a new nobility, a new purpose.

There is, however, a variety of models, a variety of forms, in which this Christian inspiration of the university finds expression in different countries and cultures. The model or form chosen partly depends upon the needs of a given culture and upon the opportunities a given culture makes available. Within the span of years of my presidency of Boston College from 1972 to 1996, the model of the Catholic university that had largely been prevalent in the United States was both challenged and reinforced, was questioned and positively refined. And as the needs of its student populations, the declining numbers of priest and religious scholars, the urgency for professionalization of governance and management, the professionalization of scholarship itself, the theological transformation emanating from Vatican II took hold, the model itself of Catholic universities in America began to change.

Each of these factors that contributed so dramatically to change during my presidency will continue to exercise their influence in the future. The form, therefore, in which the American Catholic university takes shape will continue to evolve, although it is unlikely that the rate of change will soon again match the transformations occasioned by the professionalization of managerial and academic activities and the change in Vatican II's theological perspective that characterized the late '60s through the '80s.

The Search for Wisdom—A Collegiate or an Individual Quest?

September 11, 1999

*Immanuel Kant framed the questions of wisdom
quite simply: What can a person know? What is worth doing?
What can a man or woman reasonably hope for?*

P RESIDENT FLYNN, CHAIRMAN Irish, friends all of Millikin University:

Each new season in life brings with it a new blend of sentiments. For President Thomas Flynn, but also in a special way for everyone with close ties to Millikin University, all eyes are fixed today not on the past, but on the future—a future that does not exist as yet and so must be a product of your imagination and creativity. Inauguration day marks a season of hope and of aspiration and of new beginnings.

There is a reason why it is a special privilege for me to join you in sharing the hope and aspiration that accompany Dr. Thomas Flynn's inauguration here as president of Millikin University [in Decatur, Illinois]. When I stood in Tom's shoes, beginning the first of my 24 years as president of Boston College, a younger Tom was not only one of our most accomplished students; he was the elected president of our 8,000 undergraduates' student government. Nineteen seventy-two was a year when students held extraordinary degrees of participation not merely in student governments, but in university-wide decision making. In my 24 years as president, I can think of no student leader who brought to that role a more balanced and responsible perspective, or who took better advantage of that experience to deepen his sense of balance and good judgment, than Tom Flynn. For the past 25 years, I have followed his career with high expectations. I am happy to extend in person my congratulations and best wishes to Tom and to the entire Board of Trustees and faculty of Millikin University on his appointment as president.

If today's inauguration is a time of hope and aspiration, if it awakens the realization that the future of Millikin University will be your and Tom's creation, what more evocative theme can we have for our ceremony than the theme of wisdom?

It is reputation for wisdom that gives authority to the teacher and wins allegiance to the leader of the community. Wisdom is a revered concept in virtually every religious tradition in the world. Independently of any religious tradition, Plato so exalted the idea of wisdom that he made its pursuit the highest form of human existence (as well as the indispensable prerequisite for successful governance).

But if religious literature has given us the most attractive, poetically compelling portrayal of wisdom, it was perhaps Aristotle that gave us the best analytic tools to understand it. According to that analysis, wisdom comes in two forms: It is the broad view that gives depth and perspective and context to all we know. It is an understanding of the world of our experience in relation to its ultimate origins and antecedents. Wisdom in this sense provides insight into each generation's questioning about the ultimate meaning of self and of world and of life itself.

It is to these same questions about ultimate meaning of self and world and life that virtually every religious tradition brings a response, believing that God intervened in history to communicate God's wisdom about the ultimate meaning of human existence and of the worlds we experience and create.

But there is a second, related form of wisdom that is of special significance on Inauguration day. It is the wisdom that brings our ultimate meanings and values to bear on the individual situations of our everyday lives. Aristotle had a special Greek word for it, *phronesis*, that we translate as practical wisdom; Aquinas named it *prudentia*—but as it appears in the earliest religious literature we translate it as simply "wisdom" *tout court.*

This wisdom is the kind of knowledge we employ not as speculative thinkers, but as decision makers, as persons with responsibilities to fulfill. When faced with alternative, seemingly competitive claims upon us, it is the knowledge that guides our free choices, that enables us to choose the course of action that is morally right and that is pragmatically successful. Clearly, it is this type of wisdom—the insight into what is the right thing to do in difficult cases of conduct—that we most closely look for in the president and that is expressed in our reading today.

The relevance of wisdom to the undertakings of our new president is rightfully foremost in our prayerful readings this morning. For in inaugurating him as president, Millikin University inaugurates as well, a new era in its own life. And if the broad outline of that era is discernible in the university's mission statement and strategic plans, the university's quality and lifestyle, its vitality and its success will depend on the imagination and wise judgment, goodwill, and dedicated effort of many of you in this room.

But if wisdom is so important a hope for the success of a university president, what role should it play in the life of the university itself, as it pursues its high mission?

This is a difficult question—almost too large and complex a question to raise in this setting. (And yet it is a question that is being asked in widening circles both outside academia and from within.) For the questions to which wisdom responds are perhaps the most searching we can ask. Immanuel Kant, the great German philosopher, framed the questions of wisdom quite simply: What can a person know? What is worth doing? What can a man or woman reasonably hope for? These are the questions to which religious faiths, over the centuries, have likewise addressed their wisdom. But precisely because that wisdom derived from religious faith, they are questions before which American universities, both public and private, have, over the course of this century, grown increasingly silent.

There are signs, however, that that silence is beginning to seek a new voice. Wellesley College, one of the distinguished women's colleges in Massachusetts, recently hosted a national conference on religious pluralism and spirituality in American higher education with the theme of exploring not whether, but how spirituality can be introduced into higher education. Organizers expected a largely regional audience with representatives from perhaps 20 universities. The last count registered 800 people from more than 350 colleges and universities with 30 of their presidents in attendance. "Our educational process has really led to the separation of the life of the mind and the life of the whole person, including the spirit," said the chancellor of one of the public university campuses in Massachusetts. "The pendulum swung so far toward a secular orientation that universities seemed to emphasize that we have no ethics, no values, no beliefs, and I think we are realizing that that kind of attitude does a serious disservice to our students and to society," said the woman president of another private institution in the same state.

Whatever success can be expected over time from the Wellesley conference and its more local sequels, every university approach to imparting wisdom must be marked with sincere humility and circumspection. Plato regarded wisdom so lofty and difficult an attainment that one could legitimately claim to love wisdom, but never to possess it. And the wisdom embodied in every religious tradition is only personally meaningful through the gift of religious faith, a gift that is not the university's to impart. Even practical wisdom cannot, strictly speaking, be taught. The almost unanimous judgment of history has been that practical wisdom, knowing what is right and will work effectively in a given situation, calls for an intuitive eye, gained not from scholarship but from experience. And even more importantly, Aristotle insisted and religious traditions concur that in order to see what is right, the wise person must want what is right.

As Millikin opens a new era—with humility and circumspection—what part will wisdom play in its future?

When I was preparing to come to Decatur, the president's office sent me a packet of materials to familiarize me with the university. In the attractive brochure sent to every incoming student, the university identifies the precise element that makes a Millikin education distinctive. And here I quote: "Working closely with … faculty, each student will be assisted in developing a plan of study that will bring him or her closer to answering three core questions …. Who am I? How can I know? What should I do?" Millikin's questions to each of its students are almost exact parallels of the questions Immanuel Kant posed in seeking wisdom: "What can a person know? What is worth doing? What can a man or woman reasonably hope for?" Millikin University courageously but modestly invites each of its students to do no less than undertake or deepen their quest for wisdom.

It is not only for President Thomas Flynn, then, but for each and every student and for the entire university that with him plots its future, that we pray for an enduring and deepened share of wisdom. And I voice that prayer in the words of Solomon, who viewed his leadership not as aggrandizement of self, but as service to others through the gift of wisdom:

"The Lord appeared to Solomon in a dream at night. God said, 'Ask something of me and I will give it to you.' Solomon answered … 'Oh Lord my God, you have made me your servant, king to succeed my father David; but I am a mere youth not knowing at all how to act. I serve you in the midst of the people whom you have chosen, a people so vast that it cannot be numbered or counted. Give your servant, therefore, an understanding heart to distinguish right from wrong ….' So God said to him: 'Because you have asked for this—not for a long life for yourself, nor for riches, nor for the life of your enemies, but for understanding so that you may know what is right—I do as you requested. I give you a heart so wise and understanding that there has never been anyone like you up to now, and after you there will come no one to equal you.'"

Liberal Education
and Educated Liberty

June 2, 1975

The measure of personal authenticity for all, is to be found in action,
in the quality of one's choices, the exercise of one's
properly understood "liberty."

I T   H A S   B E E N   almost a decade since Daniel Bell wrote
his landmark summary of the recent history of liberal education in America, and provided what he hoped would be
the blueprint for the reformation of programs to revitalize
the liberally educative mission of undergraduate colleges
and universities. His historical reading of the lofty inten-
tions and ambitious curricula that had characterized the
University of Chicago, Columbia, and Harvard, found each of
these programs by 1966, "reduced to a junkyard of unrelated
fragments."

The pressures that had weakened the vitality of liberal education in these institutions, we are all familiar with: pressures upward from the high schools and downward from the
graduate faculties; pressures from a growingly professionalized and differentiated society in which specialized skills
are a condition of entrance and mobility; and within the
undergraduate college itself, the increasing specialization,
departmentalization, and consequent isolation of faculty
members and their offerings. Under the centrifugal pressure
of departmental specializations, coherence and unity in programs of liberal education broke down, and perhaps the best

that remained was a distribution requirement to guarantee at least a certain breadth to a young man or woman's education, as counterweight to the increasing depth of his or her specialization.

Bell proposed his own remedies for what he considered a sorry situation. And since he wrote in 1966, literally shelves of literature have appeared on the goals and means of communicating liberal education. Almost every treatment of the subject, however, begins as does my own, with the rueful observation that the state of liberal education is indeed in disarray. Ingenious individuals create immensely profitable courses; and by dint of extraordinary effort, professors from differing departments succeed in forging illuminating interdisciplinary courses. But the colleges themselves, as colleges, remain virtually speechless in articulating any coherent rationale identifying the purpose of their liberal education. Even if successful in articulating a collegiate purpose that is more than artful language, most major colleges must acknowledge in honesty that this philosophic unity dissolves in the hardheaded task of creating curricular programs to guarantee its achievement.

I would like to affirm more, however, than the fact that American colleges have difficulty in articulating a unified rationale for liberal education, and in planning curricula to carry it into practice. I suggest that American higher education proceeds from a presupposition that makes such difficultly inevitable—and, as long as the same presupposite remains at work, inescapable.

This presupposite, quite simply, is that liberal education is directed almost exclusively at the intellects of students; that it is the communication of truths and skills and habits and qualities of intellect—as though keenness and method in knowing and voluminousness in one's learning constitutes one liberally educated.

But so long as "knowledge" remains the exclusive focus of liberal education, and so long as fields of knowledge continue to differentiate and expand in specialized refinement, the more impossible will it become to select content and methods that provide a coherently liberalized curriculum. If specialization, even within the humanities, creates more highly refined knowledge, our problem can only become increasingly insoluble, our selection of curriculum more arbitrary.

What is sorely needed to break out of this vicious circle is to establish a reference point outside of knowledge itself, to serve as magnetic "north" in defining liberal education's purpose, and in setting guidelines for the curriculum to achieve it. After all, the *artes liberales* were originally the arts and habits befitting a person who is free.

But to set the purpose of education outside of knowledge, would we not be abandoning an insight shared by all of Western culture since Aristotle—that knowledge is a good in itself, worth pursuing for its own sake? Would we not be abandoning the intellectualist view of man that came from Aristotle through Aquinas, to shape centuries of intellectualist humanism: that the highest good for man is truthful knowledge because, as Aristotle put it, "Man is *nous*—man is mind."

It would be difficult to overestimate the educational consequences of this simple expression of the philosophic nature of the human person and the identification of his highest good. If it is once agreed upon or presupposed that the good life of a man or a woman is a life of mind, that the highest good for the human person is the contemplation of truth, defining the goals and curricula of liberal education shifts to the universe of knowledge itself in the search for those fields and those methodologies that will best fulfill the potentialities of mind.

Influential as this intellectualist conception of the human

person has been in our cultures, I do not expect that upon examination any one of us fully believes it. Indeed, scholars recognize that despite the seeming clarity of Aristotle's words just quoted, they are a radical oversimplification of his understanding of the complexity of human nature and of its true good. It certainly does not express the Jewish or Christian biblical view of human fulfillment. It is too narrow to embrace the insights of continental philosophies of the person, and of action, that have radically transformed our philosophic view of ourselves in the last hundred years.

I do not feel I need belabor the point that in Jewish and Christian biblical tradition, the measure of a man or a woman was never to be found in the magnitude of one's intellectual attainments. That measure was to be found rather in how sensitively, how responsively, one exercised his or her freedom. The great Commandment is: Thou shall love the Lord thy God with thy whole heart and mind and soul, and thy neighbor as thyself.

Though the accents of love wax and wane, parallel emphasis on the exercise of freedom as the touchstone of human fulfillment runs from Marx to Marcel, from Blondel to Ricoeur. Granted the radical differences among each of these thinkers, the measure of personal authenticity for all is to be found in action, in the quality of one's choices, the exercise of one's properly understood "liberty." Contemporary man's philosophic view of himself has shifted from that of thinker to that of free and responsible source of initiative and of action. I believe it is time our philosophy of liberal education reflected that shift.

I would assert quite simply that the final test of the civilizing process that is liberal education is to be found more accurately in the quality of choices one makes during life than in evidence of purely intellectual attainments. The specific purpose of such a liberal education should be to enable persons, to the extent that formal education can do so, to make sound human decisions affecting both personal lives and social policies.

To cast the same thought in another form, Gabriel Marcel says that the basic problem of reality is not that of being and nothingness—but of the empty and the full, of richness and impoverishment. The critical test of human fulfillment and of liberal education is of the same order: It is no mere question of speculative knowing or not knowing; It is a question of richness or emptiness of life that are the direct fruits of free decisions more than of our knowledge.

I want, however, to correct immediately a misunderstanding that my words could easily generate. In making certain types of choice, the goal and hopefully end result of liberal education, I am not attempting to assert the greater importance of will over against reason. Still less am I embracing some form of anti-intellectualism, or sacrificing education to pietistic or unenlightened social activism. My point rather is that the university, in its efforts at liberal education, has a responsibility toward both intellect and liberty, and that the development of each, even for the 18-year-old, is relevant to the other.

Fundamentally, my position is a simple one. Liberal education should aspire, at its deepest level of intention, to educate for the enriching and constructive exercise of liberty. Without predetermining any particular curriculum, such an intention deriving from outside the universe of knowledge supplies not only a rationale for including certain disciplines within a curriculum, but a perspective that will lend distinctiveness to each discipline's treatment. This rationale, however, is by no means rigid or inflexible in its adaptability to a wide range of alternative curricula. If it counsels some disciplines as peculiarly relevant to certain types of human choices, it invites an infinite variety of ways of making any of the humanities, the natural or social sciences, illuminating for man's task of freedom.

Before closing, I would like to make one brief observation on some recent trends in higher education that, I believe, indicate that collegiate interest in human freedom is just below the surface of the exclusive intellectualism that has framed so much of our educational theory. On every side, one hears and reads and witnesses pledges of institutional interest in values, in interdisciplinary courses, in the future. Whether or not each institution avowing these interests will have the consensus necessary to act effectively upon these pledges, one can only wait and see. But I feel certain that unless they somehow find a footing in the theory of education of institutions, they will prove no more than fads as passing as those of the '60s. We are not, after all, very far from the days when some of our most eminent educators could insist that the university is exclusively concerned with the research and communication of knowledge, and that value considerations must be sought in other agencies of society.

If one affirms, however, that constructive, enriching, and responsible exercise of freedom is the goal of liberal education, then values enter of necessity and on an equal footing with truth, into the university's province.

Furthermore, when the human person brings knowledge to bear on choices to be made in public policy or private life, insights germane to the decision usually comes from a synthetic interweaving of understanding from different disciplines. Ethics, economics, psychology, political theory may all have their contribution to make in the effective resolution of a state's budgetary crisis, to cite one example. An academic program that looks to choice, therefore, should be naturally inclined to fashion certain interdisciplinary courses that effect a synthesis of learning from diverse academic fields.

Lastly, though deliberation toward human choice profits

from historical experience, choice is always a not-yet; deliberation is always future oriented. For the person who would use freedom well, therefore, means should be found to make the horizon of the future as familiar and as real to him as the lessons of the past. And because human decisions, as the goal of liberal education, are both in the future and are free, liberal educators must remain modest in their aspirations—aware that the achievement of their goal depends as much on their students as on themselves.

Truth of Heart

May 19, 2001

It is as though the university drew a curtain
between mind and heart, between intellectual discovery
and commitment, with each irrelevant to the other.

I N T H E S E S P L E N D I D surroundings, even a cloudy morning cannot mar the glory of this occasion. Hopes for this day began years ago in homes near at hand and in many distant places. Today those dreams are coming true.

Let me begin by extending to all of the welcome parents and family members of our graduates my very special tribute of admiration and respect. The diplomas awarded today will indeed carry the names of your sons and daughters, but they will also bear the seal of your understanding and encouragement, of your sacrifice and your love.

To you the graduates, I am happy to convey not only my congratulations, but also my pride in standing with you as a degree recipient in the Class of 2001 of a sister Jesuit university. It is a privilege to share this day with you. Even more daunting for each of you, than for me, is the realization that today is not merely the insertion of a marker between the pages of a book that you will return to at a later date. Today you close the covers of that book. During the course of 24 years as a university president, I had the privilege of conferring some 75,000 baccalaureate and master's and doctoral degrees. That experience helped me understand there is no metaphor adequate to express the sentiments each of you are experiencing this morning; to help us sort out the mix of elation and nostalgia, of satisfaction and new ambition that is everywhere among us.

During the past few weeks, I am sure that each of you graduating seniors relived many of the experiences that made these years so richly enjoyable. I shall not attempt this morning to re-create memories of those four years. Your president, Fr. Graham, did that with extraordinary eloquence at the baccalaureate Mass last evening. In these few moments I would like to reflect with you, not on another lesson in economics or world politics or in art, but rather on the message of the university itself.

For beyond all the academic lessons that you have learned so well, there has been a silent message in these classrooms and hushed libraries—a message that is not the object of any discipline or department, but that has the power to color every frame of the future that will be yours.

Indeed, the most fundamental message of the university is not audible in words. But that message is the inspiration that raised the walls of these buildings decades ago. It is the same message that is graphically displayed by all of us as we assemble on this glorious spring day. Our presence on this campus is a massive affirmation of the importance of human intelligence and of the importance of developing it. For all of you and your families, that affirmation has entailed a significant financial investment. But even more, it has meant an investment of yourself—of your precious years and energies and interests—in expanding your intellectual powers as broadly and deeply, and at times as narrowly and precisely, as your professors asked of you.

This respectful recognition of the importance of human intelligence that is the first message of the university was captured for me in a very striking way years ago in three short words of the great Medieval saint and scholar, Bonaventure.

His words were "*intellectum valde ama*." Love your own mind mightily. Most striking was his choice of verb—mightily *love* your own mind. It is among your noblest gifts and source of personal dignity. It is the light that has guided our path from the beginnings of human civilization to the information age. And despite the celebrity of instant millionaires and overnight media stars of your age, there is no greater human asset you can gain today than the academic degree you are receiving.

But a university is more than a chilly monument to intelligence; its success depends upon it being a community of scholars. As you sought out your places in the procession this morning, I know each of you recognized that your dreams and hopes for today have been realized through the friendship and support you have given to each other. A sense of community within a university, one never sees listed as a key objective or goal. And yet it is the soil in which your education grew; and it will be an indispensable key to unlock your hopes of the future. This sense of community that all of you have created and each of you has shared is part of the genius of Xavier University.

Admittedly, you cannot take these handsome turrets or the air you breathed at Xavier University with you tomorrow. Yet if you are going to address the challenge that will surface in every aspect of living, from the intimacy of family to the complexity of global business, you must take Xavier's sense of community with you. From a president's perspective, it is the mortar that makes the college a college; for you, it is the lifeblood that has given confidence and enthusiasm to all you have accomplished in your years on this campus.

At the same time that your diploma today seals you as a graduate, there is one final message that diploma conveys. Surely, the primary factor responsible for your choosing Xavier was the quality of its academic programs. And yet the society you enter tomorrow will expect more of you than a finely trained mind. For all its nobility, it is not intelligence alone that makes the world go 'round. Something else does. Love, fidelity, belief, trustworthiness, courage, fairness to others, and a capacity for sacrifice—these give meaning and depth to friendship and family and career. But surely these are not the business of a university. Or are they?

During the past several years, even the past several months, a number of penetrating studies have appeared that have attempted to draw a portrait not merely of you, the graduates of today's colleges, but a portrait of the impact or the message that universities have communicated to you. On the one hand, your portrait is remarkably positive. Your generation of graduating seniors, we are told, "have benefited from all the … instruction and opportunities with which the country has provided them. [Today's graduates] are responsible, they are generous, they are bright, they are good natured." But this same author, after weeks of interviewing students on their campus, concludes that today's universities "impose all sorts of rules to reduce safety risks and encourage achievement. They do not go to great lengths to build character the way … adult institutions did a century ago." To continue the quote, "When it comes to character and virtue, young people have been left on their own. Today's educational institutions work frantically … to foster good study skills, to promote musical talents. We fly our children around the world so that they can experience different cultures. We spend huge amounts of money on safety equipment and sports coaching … But when it comes to character and virtue, the most mysterious area of all, suddenly the *laissez-faire* ethic rules; you're on your own, Jack and Jill, go figure out what is true and just for yourselves." The author who penned these lines concludes that if today's graduates "are indeed running the country in a few decades, we'll be in fine shape. It will be a good country, though maybe not a great one" ("The Organization Kid" by David Brooks, *The Atlantic Monthly*, April 2001).

These critical comments of today's university students are not new. But, in my view, they are not an accurate portrait of you; they are not an accurate portrait of Xavier. What is true is that during much of the past halfcentury, even some of the best private universities have declared, at times in the words of their deans and presidents, that even though love and fidelity and justice and courage may make the world go 'round, knowledge is the only value appropriate for the university's mission. Other values, of a moral or ethical nature, may be the responsibility of the family or of the church, but not of the university, which stands valuationally neutral. It is as though the university drew a curtain between mind and heart, between intellectual discovery and commitment, with each irrelevant to the other.

But this is not the message universities conveyed over the long, seven-century history of their existence. It has not been the message of this university. It is true that in the mysterious gift of freedom each of you possesses, only you can ultimately shape the features of your character. But both in institutional policy and in day-to-day practice, Xavier University has persistently attempted to assist you in cultivating the mature sensibilities of your whole person—to equip you not only for professional success, but to assist you in finding meaning that goes beyond mere measures of technical competence or financial rewards. And although the pedagogies for assisting you in setting your compass by certain values are different from the pedagogies to understand chemistry or marketing or literature, it is the maturing of your personality around a set of values that has been one of this university's highest aspirations for you. It is the set of values that will give direction and motive power and ultimately satisfaction to the manner in which you use your gifts of intelligence and training.

Neither this university nor I have any blueprint to the challenges and opportunities of the new millennium in which you will live your adult lives. In the 24 years I served as university president, I bade farewell to graduates entering a world cloaked in the menacing dangers of Vietnam, a world of discouraging economic recessions, the world of exhilarating hope from the collapse of the Berlin Wall. Whatever your personal Vietnam or your personal walls whose collapse opens new horizons, if Xavier inspired you to deepen your appreciation of the gifts of intelligence gratuitously given you, I am confident you will create your own blueprint or break a new path, or find a better way than we could have prescribed for you.

So even today, as you close your formal course of studies at Xavier University, the university repeats its persistent message: a message of respect for the power and light of intelligence in all of human life, a message of confidence that as knowledge has grown within this community of scholars, the indispensable ingredient of friends will be present in all we do; and Xavier University's final message that, however important quantitative measures of intellectual talent, they will never be our measure, or the world's ultimate measure of you. Our measures will include the larger scales of justice, and love and courage in the world that you create. To paraphrase our author, I am convinced that, if you are indeed running the country in a few decades, and you will be, we'll be in fine shape. It will be not only a good country, thanks to you it will be a great one. Congratulations!

Perspective on Jesuit Education

May 25, 1986

*Two ideas, the nobility of intellect and faith, and the continuity
between them, form the horizon within which
every Jesuit school exists.*

F<small>R. CALLAHAN</small>, M<small>ISTER</small> Chairman of the Board of
Trustees, distinguished faculty, graduates of the class of 1986,
parents, family, and friends of the graduates: It is a distinct
honor for me to address the 1986 graduating class of Boston
College High School. If the traces of maroon and gold, and
the symbolic eagle, and the family name of the institution,
were not sufficient to make me feel thoroughly at home on
this occasion, the memory of my own graduation from a Jesuit high school—despite the distance of time and place—
make this occasion a very welcome homecoming for me. And
perhaps the fact that I have traveled the same paths as the
graduates makes me especially appreciative of what you have
accomplished, and makes my congratulations to you thoroughly sincere.

I would like, this afternoon, however, to extend my congratulations beyond the accomplishments of the graduates,
to include your mothers and fathers who are present in the
audience. If graduation from Boston College High School is
a singular academic accomplishment, and it is, it has come
about not only through the talent and dedication of the
graduates, but through the singular initiative of their parents. I say "initiative," because other forms of education were

clearly available that would have involved less financial sacrifice and much less human cost. It is a testimony to your love for your children, and a testimony to your appreciation of the importance of the education available at Boston College High School, that you encouraged your son to pursue his education at this institution.

Graduation from high school is genuinely one of life's dramatic transitions. In terms of personal development, graduation coincides, for most students, with the transition from adolescence to young manhood. Academically, the conclusion of high school means that, in breadth and depth, the groundwork is now in place for what can be legitimately recognized as higher education. And in terms of human relationships, graduation from high school is the first significant break with close friendships that have been the fabric of so much of your young life, and it marks the recognition within your family that a new form of self-reliance is to be expected. Because commencement is a time of transition, it is a time to savor accomplishments past, and anticipate excitement that lies ahead.

But for these brief moments this afternoon, I want to recommend that we leave for tomorrow the dreams of the colleges you will attend, the careers you will pursue, and the new friends you will meet. I fear that we spend so much time in anticipating the future that we do not prepare well enough for it by surveying the ground on which we stand, and savoring today's brilliant accomplishments that make a future possible.

Tomorrow, you will go your different ways, to different homes, different jobs, different colleges, and different vocations. What is your common legacy that you take with you as graduates of Boston College High School? What is the common prize that has become yours, the source of family resemblance that will mark you as in some sense brothers, no matter what the course of your future education?

I am sure that from one perspective, each member of the class could answer that question in much more rich detail, and with more vivid examples, than I. Obviously, by any standard of evaluation, you have gained an academic education that ranks among the best; perhaps not through your own choosing, you have gained an appreciation of the richness and precision of language that is the indispensable key to progress in all learning. You have taught yourselves how to direct your energies and talents to best effect, and the curriculum you have studied has not only introduced you to new vantage points for seeing the world, it has also given you the first sound evidence of the breadth of your own intellectual gifts, and where they can most effectively be employed. For those of you who have taken ample advantage of the extra-curriculars, you have attained a degree of art and skill, but above all of self-confidence, that will be invaluable allies in making your gifts of intelligence productive.

But in a sense, all of this, though true, is inadequate to catch the mystique of your own educational legacy. You do not capture the spirit of a family by describing its external features or the regime of activities they customarily follow. And you will not fully understand the legacy of your Boston College High School education simply by reviewing the curriculum and recalling the rigors of the exam schedule or the nostalgia of your many happy times together.

Boston College High School shares a patrimony with 47 other Jesuit high schools in the United States, and with Jesuit high schools around the world. It is a sister institution to the 28 Jesuit colleges and universities in America, and scores more throughout the world. These institutions have existed in almost every one of the world's cultures, at every level of instruction, from high school to post-doctoral research, and are frequented by students who share the system for one or four or 11 or more years.

Last November, the newly elected General of the Jesuits convened a meeting to discuss the mission of Jesuit education with 100 presidents of Jesuit higher educational institutions from around the world. In addition to my 27 colleagues from the United States, there were presidents from Beirut and Mexico and India and Brazil and Spain and Taiwan and Manila and Nicaragua. Our institutions enrolled a half-million students and represented the investment in lives of some 4,500 Jesuits and 45,000 lay faculty and staff. High school students in the United States alone add an additional 40,000 to the totals attending Jesuit educational institutions. In India, in Japan, at St. Joseph's in Beirut and Sogang in Korea, vast numbers of students and faculty, in some cases the majority, are not Catholics, indeed, are not Christians. If the numbers in themselves are not important, the sheer diversity of these Jesuit educators, of every race and color, working in a dozen different cultures and at every level of academic attainment, says much about Jesuit education, about Boston College High School, and about the legacy you men take from this platform wherever you go.

In countries where public education is abundant, and in countries plagued by poverty and oppression, why would this order of religious priests invest so much of its human capital in teaching and administration of the arts and literatures and sciences, in Taiwan and Boston and Calcutta and Rio, with collaborators who are, in many cases, of radically different religious beliefs? There is no simple answer to this question, and yet there is an answer, more eloquently dramatized by what these institutions do, than by what they say about themselves in catalogues and bulletins and curricula. The answer lies in the belief in two ideas, which cannot be proven or demonstrated, but which lie at the foundation of every Jesuit school and are the legacy of every Jesuit graduate, no matter what his future education, no matter what his adult career.

The first is the belief that the profusion of the literatures and arts and musics and political theories, the diversity within culture and cultures, are the flowering of the human spirit, and have a validity and worth that enriches the human family. Gothic architecture and Shakespeare's sonnets and Plato's *Republic* did not exhaust the creative insight of the human spirit, but they contributed richly to the advance of human culture. The Jesuit school exists to share an appreciation of the illuminating power of each of these, and also to stimulate its students and scholars to enrich life further through their own insights and artistry.

The second is the belief in the unity and continuity between the humanism of the world's cultures and Christianity itself. If faith alone mattered to human destiny, if church and religious belief were sufficient to themselves, there would be no Jesuit school committed to the understanding of Greek literature or trigonometry or microbiology or supply-side economics. And if the sum of all these were adequate to explain the meaning of human existence and to constitute human fulfillment, there would be no need for a Jesuit school that believes human culture is incomplete without the grace of faith and love that come not from human contriving, but as God's gift; no need for a Jesuit school that believes that it is only from the respectful and serene dialogue of faith and culture that a genuinely richer culture will result.

These two ideas, the nobility of intellect and faith, and the continuity between them, form the horizon within which every Jesuit school exists. They are the patrimony which should enrich every Jesuit school graduate. They should be your lasting inheritance, more than the facility with Greek grammar or differential equations or American history that might appear today your most cherished accomplishment.

These two ideas that underlie Jesuit schools create an attitude and impose an obligation. The attitude is one of love and of supreme confidence; St. Bonaventure could have been inscribing the diploma of every Jesuit graduate when he said "*Intellectum valde ama*," love your own mind mightily. And if you love your mind, you will trust it. You will never fear its discoveries.

But the idea that is the legacy of the Jesuit graduate also poses an obligation. The unity of an enlightened faith and the world's cultural advances is not automatic, is not an achievement of some century past, or some year of your own development. It is a unity that arises from the ongoing dialogue of faith and culture that is the role of the Jesuit school to host and the task of the Jesuit graduate to continue.

Your talent, your faith, your confidence, and Boston College High School have prepared you well for that dialogue to continue, and I wish you Godspeed in carrying it out.

Jesuit Higher Education and Ignatian Spirituality

June 7, 1989

We can ease the persistent tension between the sacred and the secular, provide a more fundamental matrix for the Jesuitness in our universities, to the extent that we attempt a new form of sharing with our lay colleagues—sharing the outlook and the intentionality that constitutes the root of Ignatian spirituality: the incarnational outlook whereby we are capable of seeing God in all things.

I AM GOING TO begin my remarks today with a brief quotation. The text is not from Scripture but from a letter I received almost exactly 30 years ago from a person many of you knew and admired, Fr. Gustave Weigel. At the time, I was pursuing a doctorate in Louvain. In his letter, Gus wrote, "If you study philosophy solely for its apostolic value to you as a priest, it will make you a poor philosopher and a poor apostle; if you study philosophy for its own intellectual validity, you will have the possibility of being a respectable philosopher and of being more effective in your ministry as a Jesuit priest." Fr. Weigel expressed an irony that all of us in higher education have experienced. It is an irony that affects our identity and perhaps the identity of our higher educational institutions; an irony that has its origin—but also its creative resolution—in Jesuit spirituality.

What I should like to do in the few moments available to me this afternoon at the Jesuit Assembly in Washington,

D.C., is to provide a very hasty sketch of some of the major changes that have taken place in our colleges and universities since Gus Weigel wrote me that letter, and on the basis of that sketch provide one formulation of the problematic that faces our universities today and indicate that, as Ignatian spirituality gave original shape to this ministry of higher education, that spirituality has unique resources to resolve the problematic of our current circumstances.

When Fr. Paul Reinert became head of the Jesuit Educational Association in 1966, he reported on university problems facing the Society of Jesus today. He singled out first and foremost "the large question of the right of the lay faculty to have a voice in establishing policy" (Paul A. FitzGerald, S.J., *The Governance of Jesuit Colleges in the United States 1920–1970*, Notre Dame Press, 1984, p. 197). Fr. Reinert pointed to the need for reorganization in structure so that Jesuits would be appointed to the faculty with the involvement of their departments and to the need for the autonomous status of the universities vis-à-vis ecclesiastical authorities. Insofar as this last item touched upon the ultimate governance responsibility for the university, its Board of Trustees, Fr. Reinert's report in 1966 foreshadowed the entire pattern of reorganization of our institutions both internally and in relation to ecclesiastical superiors in the Society. These changes constituted the adoption of policies of tenure and of academic freedom and due process, the recognition of faculty prerogatives in the formation of academic policy, and at the board level, the independence in governance from jurisdictional authority, either of the Church or of Jesuit superiors. This autonomy always existed *de jure*. But the election of majorities of lay trustees, first to the Board of Saint Louis University and then to almost all of our institutions, dramatized that autonomy and stimulated the separate incorporation of our religious communities that formalized the independent status and prerogatives of each.

For my intent in this talk, however, more important than the changes themselves, which are very familiar to you, is the interpretation of their purpose and end result. In his book on the subject, Fr. Paul FitzGerald referred to this process as the Americanization of Jesuit colleges and universities (FitzGerald, *ibid*). However valid this perspective, I believe it is more important to conceive the change not in political or nationalistic terms but to recognize that the process was a conscious effort to meet the evolving standards of quality established by peer institutions of higher education. Those professional standards themselves were not formulated out of thin air or developed arbitrarily. They were responses to the demands of increasing complexity in our institutions, to the evolution of the academic disciplines through a genuine knowledge explosion, and to the increased capabilities that advances in the professional disciplines made possible. To that extent, academic freedom, peer involvement of faculty in appointments, promotion, and policymaking, independence in governance from civil and ecclesiastical authorities—as was made clear recently in Rome—are not American standards. For the most part they are standards of professional quality for the academy itself, everywhere, and will be the conditions of professional standing and influence into the next century.

The story of these changes, of course, is a story of statesmanship and vision, of pragmatic idealism and of sacrifice. Despite all of the extensive reflections this interesting process stimulates, I simply point out that the end result, and in large measure the purpose of this many-sided professionalization of our universities, was the creation of immensely richer forms of collaboration and partnership between Jesuits and lay men and women colleagues. Clearly partnership between

Jesuits and lay colleagues in the operation of colleges is not a new phenomenon. To employ one of the philosopher Gabriel Marcel's perspectives, however, collaboration is a notion that is not simply present or absent in an organization; it is susceptible of relatively richer or poorer meanings—meanings that are empty or full. And today, among Jesuit and non-Jesuit, lay men and women, there is a sharing of functions and of fundamental responsibility for Jesuit colleges and universities that reaches from the earliest entry level faculty position to that of chairman of the Board of Trustees (with only the role of president, and that I suspect temporarily, excluded in some institutions).

And yet, as I will explain in a moment, I believe there is a level of partnership richer still that is possible, and that will enhance all other changes to date in proving ultimately successful.

I believe that the very form of our contemporary problematic, as many people frame it, points to its solution—and to the source of its solution in Ignatian spirituality.

By and large, no one contests whether Jesuit colleges and universities are stronger today—academically, managerially, in research capability, in the quality of our faculties and graduates. Their question rather is whether institutional excellence is at the expense of Jesuit character and identity. Because of the declining number of Jesuits available and the independence of university governance from formal Society jurisdiction, friends ask not whether Fordham or Boston College will continue to exist, but whether they will continue to be Jesuit—and how Jesuit.

The wording of the problematic contains the clues for its solution. Let me put it in the words of President Frank Rhodes who, in his keynote address, echoed the title of our own gathering, "so long as Jesuit colleges and universities exercise a genuine *ministry* of higher education, they will be authentically Jesuit." By ministry he and we mean an activity that, whatever its cultural or humanistic worth, has a religious significance as a form of service to God.

Let me say immediately that if the professionalization and rich forms of collaboration have made the problem of Jesuit identity in colleges and universities more pressing, efforts of the past 10 years have been most fruitful in identifying characteristics or marks of Jesuit universities and in developing programs to implement them. In almost every case these characteristics and programs have been consciously derived from one or another aspect of Ignatian outlook and spirituality. Without attempting to summarize, let me simply make reference to Fr. Arthur F. McGovern's monograph, *Jesuit Education and Jesuit Spirituality (Studies in the Spirituality of Jesuits,* Sept. 1988), the 1987 booklet on *The Characteristics of Jesuit Education* (Jesuit Secondary Education Association, Washington, D.C., 1987)—and the countless activities on each of the 28 campuses I have heard recounted at our meeting of presidents.

And yet the problematic persists; indeed, it becomes more urgent as the level of professionalism and the scope of collaboration continue to increase. What we need, therefore, is a design that will do three things: (a) that will overcome the tension between the apparently secular and Jesuit identities of the university; (b) that will go beyond identifiable marks or characteristics that tend to compartmentalize the Jesuitness of an institution and, rather, lay down a matrix or fundamental inspiration capable of pervading the totality; (c) that will raise to a new level of richness the partnership between Jesuit and lay colleagues.

Perhaps it is almost a truism to say that Ignatian spirituality provides that design, that strategy. Tom Clarke very succinctly describes spirituality as a reflective perspective or organization and prioritizing of theological and ethical beliefs and principles—as well as the practical lifestyle or regime of life consonant with that perspective (Thomas E. Clarke, S.J., *Ignatian Spirituality and Societal Consciousness—Studies in the Spirituality of Jesuits*, Vol. VII, No. 4, Sept. 1975, p. 129).

Let me single out only two of the elements that shape the distinctive perspective of Ignatian spirituality—the thoroughgoing incarnational theology of Ignatius and his eminently contemporary emphasis on intentionality rather than on the material structure of human activities as constitutive of their moral goodness and worth for Jesuits.

Ignatian spirituality was clearly shaped by Ignatius's gift of "finding God in all things" that led Jerome Nadal, his astute assistant, to describe him as a "contemplative even while in action." For Ignatius "grace and revelation are verified in the whole of human experience—including human structures and institutions." In commenting on this facet of Ignatian spirituality, Tom Clarke says "it is not fanciful or romantic, but a simple consequence of [Ignatius's worldview] to find God present for example in parliamentary procedures, in a sound civil law, in the elaborate procedures of a major surgical operation" (Clarke, *loc. cit.*, p. 141)—and one could add in the successful balancing of a $200 million budget or in the conduct of an original piece of basic research "and because our human call is not only to find God already present but also, in a real sense, to make Him more perfectly present by our being the human instruments of creational and redemptional process, our being contemplatives in action will verify itself in every effort to create a better human world … every human achievement, to the degree it is genuinely and fully human, is a grace of God" (Clarke, *ibid*).

If ministry connotes relating one's actions to God, it is this Ignatian outlook that more forcefully than any other makes our entire enterprise a genuine ministry of higher education.

As I borrow one element of Ignatian spirituality from his

incarnational theology, let me take one from his view of what makes action eminently worthwhile. When Joseph de Guibert, in his monumental study, sifts through the sources and elements of Ignatian spirituality to find its one most distinguishing characteristic, he locates it not in a particular practice, or speculative principle—but he situates it rather in a motive or intention, namely the intention in all things to better serve the Lord out of passionate love (Joseph de Guibert, S.J., *Le Spiritualité de la Compagnie de Jésus*, Roma, Institutum Historicum, 1954, pp. 165–170).

Partly through the contributions of phenomenology, we have come to seek the ground of goodness in acts, not just in the material or biological structure of acts—but in their intentionality—viz., in the meaning recognized and given value in our choosing. In a very genuine sense an action is laudably Ignatian not in terms of its structural content—whether it is studying theology or preaching or teaching physics—but in its intentionality to be of greater service to God who is discernible and present in all things. To be sure, Ignatian spirituality provides manifold criteria for discerning the greater good and God's will for us—but we sometimes underestimate his radical indifference and pragmatism regarding the "intrinsic" merits of certain types of activity—in preference for the Ignatian overriding importance of the motive of serving God and the world in all we do.

I believe we are, here, at the juncture point of the sacred and the secular, at the core of the mystery of Jesuit life and professional apostolates, at the level of intentionality that makes education, or any activity, Ignatian. It is not just an ethic of intention but of intentionality, because God *is* findable in all things—but He is so findable only to the eyes of faith and perhaps only through the force of prayer.

What I am suggesting, therefore, is that we can ease the persistent tension between the sacred and the secular, provide a more fundamental matrix for the Jesuitness in our universities, to the extent that we attempt a new form of sharing with our lay colleagues—sharing the outlook and the intentionality that constitutes the root of Ignatian spirituality: the incarnational outlook whereby we are capable of seeing God in all things, and the capacity to attempt to respond in love to God in service to Him in all we do.

The programmatic for developing this new form of partnership will require much more reflection than is possible in these brief pages. I personally believe, however, that developing such a programmatic could be the most valuable, distinctive, and perhaps challenging contribution our Jesuit communities could now make to the life of "Jesuit" colleges and universities.

Let me indicate three advantages of making this new effort on the part of Jesuits. First of all, it makes us accountable for what Fr. General, back in 1985, advised the presidents—that we should be seeking as Jesuits in our institutions, not for power, but for authority; and authority comes not from what we have, but from what we are; and that what we are stems from our spirituality, from being able to find God in all things and from the desire in all we do to serve only Him and His people.

Secondly, I am convinced that this effort to share Ignatian spirituality, indeed through forms of prayer, would be responsive to the interests of many of our lay colleagues who want to realize more clearly for themselves the personal meaning and personal fulfillment of their lives in and through their professional work.

Lastly, I believe that this type of sharing of spirituality would serve more appropriately to locate Jesuit character within all functions of the institution, making all of them, as the title of our conference indicates, a "ministry" of higher education that in many ways will not be materially different from what President Rhodes's colleagues do at Cornell, but in intentionality will be radically different.

With the presence of this intentionality, I am sure that we will continually recognize new ways of pragmatically fulfilling the remaining "marks" of Jesuit identity in our institutions.

Catholic Universities
and the University Professor

February 4, 1992

*The fact is that though "born," as the
Holy Father recently expressed it, "from the heart of the Church,"
the university is a creation of human culture that possesses its own
intrinsic dynamism.*

AFTER COMPLETING 20 full years as president of a
Catholic university, I consider it a distinct compliment to be
invited to speak about the mission of Catholic higher education and the role that faculty play in accomplishing it. Some
might worry that there is an irony or perhaps even a booby
trap in inviting a president to speak on the role of faculty. I
take confidence from the fact that the large majority of those
in attendance are, like myself, no longer teaching faculty but
rather presidents.

As a matter of fact, some of you may be aware that I had
the privilege of addressing the same topic before the International Federation of Catholic Colleges and Universities in
Toulouse this past summer. It is perhaps that presentation
that occasioned my presence here this evening as it certainly
will provide much of the backdrop and some of the content
of what I have to say.

In speaking to the audience at Toulouse, I attempted to
focus upon two aspects of the faculty member's role in contributing to the Catholic character of the university. The first
had to do with the aspiration of every Catholic college and

university to assist not merely in a narrowly intellectual development of our students, but in the contribution that the university, partly through its faculty, makes in the development of the whole person. Indeed, one of the great strengths of Catholic higher education is that it rests upon an implicit philosophy or theology of the human person. In the Christian perspective, the ultimate worth of a human person is not measured merely by what we know, but rather what we freely do. While always profoundly committed to the importance of knowledge in and for itself, Catholic higher education has never regarded the human person as exclusively "thinker," but also as radically free, with knowledge instrumentally serving as a light to both the responsiveness and the creativity inherent in human freedom.

By reason of this theological perspective on the student as person, a significant purpose of Catholic higher education is to assist in the development of individuals for a creative, enlightened, and responsible exercise of their freedom. This I take to be a large overriding purpose Catholic education assumes, and it is for this reason that the personal outlook of the faculty member is so important—recognizing students not merely as minds to be sharpened, but as a story to be written, a story they will write, with God's grace, for themselves, a story of a freedom that only they can exercise, but that we can assist them with.

Admittedly, not every faculty member in every discipline will be in a position to contribute equally to this formative educational role. Through the decade of the '50s and early '60s, however, too many universities abandoned altogether any institutional effort to deal with freedom and values, not least because of their inability to establish any institutional consensus regarding values or any coherent philosophy of the human person and of the meaning of human life. But the point I would emphasize is that, given the Christian conception of the person underlying our efforts, an important part of the problematic of Catholic higher education becomes the pedagogy of freedom. And it is a pedagogy that cannot be left exclusively to officials in the student affairs areas of our colleges and universities, but needs address by the academic faculty and the curriculum of studies. The pedagogy of calculus or of economics or of Greek is relatively easy; but the pedagogy of freedom—how you understand it, how you assist it to be responsive, how you recognize its developmental stages at different chronological ages, how you enlarge its creativity, how you communicate an experience of its fundamental thrust as one of love rather than of personal aggrandizement—this is one of the fundamental tasks in educating the whole person, where our faculties have a unique opportunity and, indeed, an obligation to our own ideals to strengthen.

If one's relationship to students forms one of the major axes that orient the life of faculty members, the other axis that shapes both their commitment and their responsibility lies in the pursuit of a specific academic field. It is precisely this relationship that constitutes the faculty member's fundamental role in the college or university that I wish to reflect upon with you at some length this evening.

Let me acknowledge from the outset that over the course of the past 25 years, the responsibilities and pressures placed upon the American university professor have enormously complicated their challenge. The literal explosion of knowledge and technology that has taken place, the increasing differentiation of academic disciplines into subspecialties, the zeal for excellence that urges both institutions and individual scholars to heightened research ambitions, the increasing efforts of universities to serve their surrounding communities, and the efforts to assist students in dealing with extraordinary social changes in these years have placed heavy burdens on their lives. Within the context of a Catholic university, there are obviously a number of perspectives in which the faculty member's professionalism in his or her academic discipline can lend distinctive strength to our universities. The presence of strong theology departments in our universities that develop and communicate the meaning of Christian revelation are an obvious source of distinctive strength to the universities as well as to the Church in its developing self-understanding and relationship to the world around it. The declared purpose of Catholic universities to create a forum for an ongoing dialogue between faith and other elements of an evolving human culture opens a clear arena for faculty members to give distinctive strength to their universities in ways disregarded by most institutions.

What I would like to focus upon, specifically, however, is the contribution to the mission of the Catholic university that the faculty member makes in the primary role he or she plays in the university, namely as scholar, professor, researcher in any of the recognized academic disciplines. Perhaps nothing so clearly defines the expectations and responsibilities and personal commitment of a scholar on our faculty or, for that matter, of a professional manager, in the conduct of our university than does the degree of quality and of professional excellence that they contribute to the university's mission. The paradox is that in the process of reflecting upon the Catholic character of our universities, the professional excellence we have achieved is too often seen as, at best, irrelevant to our Catholic character and at worst, at odds with it.

Thirty years ago, those of us who witnessed the staggering investment state governments were devoting to campus facilities, to faculties and programs, believed that the maintenance of our academic standing within the higher educational community was a nearly insurmountable task. By and large, no one today questions whether Catholic colleges and universities are stronger today than ever in their past—academically, managerially, in research capability, in the quality of faculties and graduates. Their question, rather, is whether professional excellence has taken place at the expense of Catholic character and identity. Further struck by the declining number of religious and priests available and by the independence of university governance from ecclesiastical jurisdiction, friends ask not whether Georgetown or St. Louis University will continue to exist, but whether they will continue to be Catholic—and how Catholic. Of greater concern still are the occasional ecclesiastical disavowals of any interest in how strong a university is ("we don't need another Harvard") over against an interest only in how "Catholic" it is.

The regrettable implication here is that there is a radical dualism at work in Catholic universities—the one element constituting the professionally academic and managerial excellence of the institution, the other its Catholic character. This latter, its Catholic character, becomes spontaneously identified with a specific department (theology) or function (chaplaincy) or even personage (priest-president) in the university. This dualistic view creates a special vulnerability in our institutions, because it provides no role in shaping the distinctively Catholic character of the university to the large majority of our faculty, and especially of our non-Catholic faculty, in their fundamental commitment to research, scholarship, and teaching in specialized academic disciplines.

And while it is important to encourage in a special way interdisciplinary research and investigation that have direct relevance to moral values and to public policy issues, such emphases, when identified with our Catholic character, can, ironically, further marginalize the role of disinterested pursuits of academic or managerial excellence.

What is at issue in understanding the faculty's role in contributing to the Catholic character of universities is no less than the problem of conceptualizing the relationship between faith and culture, the relationship of Church and world, in a sense the relationship of nature and the supernatural.

The tendency to dualistic thinking in reflecting upon Catholic universities is as old as Christianity itself. In a few short pages of his compendium *Catholicism*, Fr. Richard McBrien (whose book was published by HarperSanFrancisco in 1994) summarizes Reinhold Niebuhr's analysis of the diverse lenses through which Christianity has historically viewed the relationship of Christ to the world. The first letter of John (McBrien, p. 383), the writings of Tertullian, the entire monastic movement in its flight from the world and clear themes in modern Protestantism view Christian life as *over against* human culture, as the antithesis of human culture. Less controversial but nonethless dualistic was the relation between the Kingdom of God and this world's kingdom of wrath and sin that is traceable from certain emphases in St. Paul up through Martin Luther to a modern expression in Reinhold Niebuhr (McBrien, p. 383 and p. 386).

My thesis tonight is that insofar as the faculty's dedication to the whole range of intellectual pursuits is almost synonymous with the world's culture, one's understanding of the academic faculty's specific contribution to the Catholic character of universities, will be a reflection of one's theological understanding of the relationship between Christian life and human culture, between Church and world, between nature and the supernatural.

Obviously, I am not going to attempt to resolve the titanic theological struggles that have taken place around each of these themes. What I would like to do in the remainder of my paper is to point up the fact that the past 50 years of theology have repeatedly emphasized a third theme as old as Christianity itself that sees Christian life achieving its end in and through the transformations of culture. Before doing this, however, I would like to take my point one step further, and assert that an understanding of the faculty's role is closely related to an understanding of the university itself—and of the transformation it has undergone in recent years.

The single most dramatic change that has taken place in Catholic colleges and universities over the years that span my personal experience of these institutions is the growing professionalism of our faculty and managerial staffs that was manifest particularly in our assimilation of professional standards of appointment and of tenure, of academic freedom and of due process to assure it, and of the confirmation of the autonomy of our institutions from ecclesiastical or religious community jurisdiction through the participation of increasing majorities of lay members of our boards of trustees. Fr. Paul FitzGerald, in his book *The History of Jesuit Colleges From the Years 1920 to 1970*, refers to this as the Americanization of the colleges and universities, though I would see the change more basically as an effort to meet standards of professional quality that are not merely American standards but are standards for the academy itself.

The fact is that though "born," as the Holy Father recently expressed it, "from the heart of the Church," the university is a creation of human culture, an element of human culture that possesses its own intrinsic dynamism or nature or laws of evolutionary growth and perfectibility that must be respected and actualized if the university is to be itself and fulfill its high promise of contributing to the cultural life of the human family. To a degree, the internal dynamic of the university is the dynamic of the human mind itself—to be self-determining in framing its inquiries, to frame hypotheses and explanations, to follow evidence, to critique accepted understanding in order to more adequately express the truth; to conduct one's scholarship in the humble recognition that the deposit of knowledge gained reflects the interdependence and critical judgment exercised among scholars themselves as both a guarantee and a safeguard of quality in one's scholarship. Indeed, it is in the mind's own innate desire to understand and in its radical responsiveness to forms of evidence that ultimately shapes the imperative of academic freedom and of autonomy that are part of the constituent nature of the university.

On the one hand, therefore, during the 10-year process that led up to the issuance of Pope John Paul II's Apostolic Constitution, *Ex Corde Ecclesiae*, most college and university people were stirred by the hope that arises from the singular promise of an institution that has achieved a full measure of cultural maturity as a university and is simultaneously Catholic. On the other side of the same coin, however, our deep concern about any repudiation of academic freedom or of institutional autonomy in the document reflected our estimate of the unwarranted tragedy that would result from any conception of Church and culture that might force a choice between our cultural imperatives as universities and our Catholic character.

Both our confidence in the newly established professional strength of our institutions and our concern for the maintenance of the integrity of academic freedom and of institutional autonomy were rooted in the belief that Christian faith and the world's culture, that full professional integrity and Catholic character in a university, are neither antithetical to each other nor evolving on dual but separate tracks. In a sense, the effort to understand the mission of a Catholic university and the effort to understand the academic faculty's specific contribution to Catholic character, are one and the same. Both depend upon some degree of success in theologically articulating what is at root a Christian mystery— the mystery of the Word's entrance into history by assuming, in its totality, human nature—and the consequent mystery of the Church's salvific mission to mankind and its culture.

Perhaps no document of the Church spoke more thematically to the relationship of the Church to the cultural forces operative in the contemporary world than Vatican II's *Gaudium et Spes.* Indeed, the positive, affirming tone and content of that document provided the impetus for much of the professionalization that has taken place in our colleges and universities over the past 25 years.

Indeed, the Council deplored as one of the most serious errors of our age the *split* between *professional* activities and *religious* life (n. 43). And while the document issues a ringing affirmation of the legitimate autonomy of human culture and especially of the sciences (n. 59), recognizes that men and women are authentic "authors of the culture" and rightly have an increasing sense of "autonomy and responsibility" (n. 55) in this endeavor, this massive affirmation of the creativity and independence and fecundity of human cultural forces, is founded, as the then-General of the Society of Jesus said, "on a mighty act of faith—in the secular, human world as the arena of God's unceasing activity" (*The University in the American Experience*, Leo McLaughlin, John Courtney Murray, and Pedro Arrupe, Fordham University Press, New York, 1966, p. 17). In a rich series of texts, the Council states and restates its incarnational perspective on *human* accomplishment as the "unfolding of the *Creator's* work," contributing "to the realization in *history* of the *divine* plan" (n. 34), an integral part of the *Christian's* vocation (n. 34), a gift and calling of the Spirit (n. 38, cf. 36). This unifying view of the scientific, cultural, and religious accomplishments of men and women, the Council, of course, grounds in Christ. "The truth is," the Council says, "that only in the mystery of the Incarnate Word does the mystery of man take on light" (p. 22, cf. 45). Consequently, that the earthly and the heavenly city penetrate each other is a fact accessible to faith alone. It remains a mystery of human history ... until the splendor of God's sons is fully revealed" (p. 40).

Whatever the truth in the historical reading of Christian life as either the antithesis of culture or in paradox to it, these perspectives are incomplete and only find their full meaning when enriched by the mission of Christ and of Christian life as the transformer of culture. "God did not send the Son into the world to condemn the world, but that the world might be saved through Him" (John 3:16–17). This was the motif that predominated in Augustine's *City of God*. As McBrien writes in *Catholicism*, "The work of culture is the work of grace and the power of grace is expressed in culture ... this world is itself destined for the Kingdom of God and we are called to facilitate its movement toward the Kingdom" (p. 387).

Perhaps no one expressed more vividly or felt more deeply the transformation of human work and most particularly the work of scholarship that the Incarnation has accomplished for the Christian believer than Pierre Teilhard de Chardin. Almost lyrically, he writes in *The Divine Milieu* (published by Harper and Row, New York, 1968) that God "awaits us every instant in our action, in the work of the moment. There is a sense in which he is at the tip of my pen, my spade, my brush, my needle—of my heart and of my thought. By pressing the stroke, the line or the stitch, on which I am engaged, to its ultimate natural finish, I shall lay hold of that last end towards which my innermost will tends" (p. 64). And even more pointedly to our topic, Teilhard writes, "I want to dedicate myself body and soul to the sacred duty of research. We must test every barrier, try every path, plumb every abyss. *Nihil intentatum* ... God wills it, who willed that he should have need of it. You are men, you say? *Plus et ego*" (pp. 69–70).

In more prosaic, but for that reason perhaps more illuminating language, Karl Rahner pointed up that despite the conceptual differences of nature and supernature, of Church and world, "… natural existence has within the concrete order of total creation, an inner openness to grace … it follows from this that everything natural, if fully and freely experienced, accepted and realized as what it really is (i.e., necessarily supernatural in its ultimate goal) is actually at every stage more than purely natural" (*The Christian Commitment*, Cecily Hastings, Karl Rahner, Sheed and Ward, New York, 1963, pp. 50–51).

Very importantly for our purposes in discussing the activities of Church-related universities, Rahner advises us not to confuse Christian life with ecclesial life: "What is ecclesial represents only a part of what is Christian, and the latter, even where it is not strictly ecclesial, is supernaturally relevant to the salvation of the individual and, above all, to the salvation and sanctification of the world. However much we may value and promote the importance, and even in certain circumstances the obligation, of participation by the laity in ecclesial life, especially in supporting and facilitating the strictly hierarchical apostolate … yet what we need above all to say and to appreciate is that the presence of Christianity and its grace does not stop at the point where outward expression of explicitly Christian and ecclesiastical life stops" (*The Christian Commitment*, pp. 67–68).

"In simple terms," Rahner adds, "Wherever in this world of men, in its economic life, in the down-to-earth reality … of its organized community life, in the whole length and breadth of individual and social life, right actions are performed, according to reality and decency, and humanity, there Christianity is achieved, even if not by that name, whether by acknowledged Christians or by others acting in this way; and hence the strictly Christian task of Christians and especially of lay Christians is fulfilled. This is not all that God demands of Christians, but it is something which he demands of them as Christians and not merely as human beings; it is the most essential element in the healing and sanctifying of the world as such" (*The Christian Commitment*, pp. 68–69).

I fear that the perspective I have been pressing may be overly abstract or theological for an evening such as this. And yet is it not, in the last analysis, the fundamental reason why the Church has been one of the most ardent supporters of the cultural reality we call the university? Is it not the fundamental reason why the Church has for so long given encouragement, and at times various forms of sponsorship, not just to religious chaplaincies or theology faculties or ethics courses or Newman Clubs—but to Catholic universities— whole faculties that, by the range and diversity and level of their intellectual resources, merit that name?

Obviously, not every faculty member, not even every Christian or Catholic faculty member, need see his or her professional contributions within this faith horizon. After all, the full reality of the unified God-Man, the full grandeur of the Church's relation to the world—and of our human vocation in Christ—are each mysteries that are grasped only in a glimpse of faith it is not ours to give. What is important is that the individual professor, whether experiencing that insight of faith or not, be given to understand that his or her apparently secular endeavors that constitute the lifeblood of university activities, are valued not less, but indeed more in the setting of a Catholic university because of their Christian significance in contributing to salvation history.

Perhaps most importantly of all, more widespread focus on this incarnational view of the university's essential thrust toward excellence in the seemingly secular arena—can create more solid ground for mutual understanding between Church officials and their neighboring Catholic universities and give new vigor to that "mutual trust, close and consistent cooperation and continuing dialogue" the Holy Father envisioned in his recent Constitution.

CHAPTER IV

FRIENDS AND
COLLEAGUES

Introduction

Among the many talks I delivered as president of Boston College, it is remarkable how many of them focused not on an educational development nor an institutional achievement, but upon the value to the College of one of its community members.

As university president, one can obviously have a powerful influence—either for good or for ill—upon the institution one leads. And yet the form of influence a president of a university exercises is more subtle than that of executives in business or government.

Surely no executive of a complex organization can be expected to generate all the creative ideas needed to bring success. Much more important is the ability to spot good ideas in others and support them; spot bad ideas and block them. One of the subtleties in the university president's role is that success will require not merely assembling an effective administrative team, but the forging of an authentic community to contribute the energies and ideas that are indispensable to forward progress.

Coming in the wake of the disruptions every college experienced from 1968 to 1972, I believe the emergence of just such a community at Boston College gave new definition to the College's possibilities and its expectations. What made the College a community was a remarkable sense of self-respect for each one's own distinctive status within the University coupled with the unifying power of common goals. From early freshman student to tenured professor, or longtime alumnus serving on a governing board, individual members of the Boston College community took the University to heart. Whether it was time or talent or energy or means that they contributed, they did not seem to look upon themselves as making a sacrifice. The academic or cultural ideals of the University, its moral or religious goals, were for many people their own personal goals as well. Whether it was a desire to give back or simply to advance an institution with which they personally could identify, not one of the successful initiatives during the 24 years of my presidency took place without the support and cooperation of either one or of an army of alumni and colleagues and close friends of the University.

To be sure, neither the type of influence contributed to the College nor the personalities of all were the same. In the following pages, I have made a selection of two classes of public presentation—talks where I had the opportunity to pay tribute and to thank individual members of the Boston College community during their lifetime, either as they were receiving recognition or honor or retiring from a longtime position—and talks where I was given the honor of being invited to speak as a priest at funeral services of graduates and colleagues and close friends all, who had served Boston College generously during their lifetimes.

Charles F. Donovan, S.J.

December 11, 1977

*His mode of leadership was a mode of encouragement to
the initiative and the resourcefulness
of all of our people.*

W E ARE GATHERED here this afternoon to honor
a distinguished alumnus of Boston College. He is a Jesuit
priest, an eloquent orator, a sage trustee and counselor at individual institutions across the face of our country. He is a
dynamic teacher, a brilliant and productive administrator,
a person each one of us immensely appreciates as a professional colleague and as a personal friend.

In the few short minutes available to me, I will not attempt
to speak for our faculties. Your presence this afternoon, the
artistic and literary expressions you have composed for the
day, eloquently express your own affection and your respect
for this great man. I do, however, want to express the gratitude of Boston College for 26 years of academic leadership to
this University. I cannot attempt to eulogize even the high
points of his years as founding dean of our School of Education, nor his 16 years as the vice president and dean of faculties for all of our academic programs.

I also want, however, to isolate an aspect of his leadership
that has characterized everything he has done; an aspect that I
believe is important because of its influence on each of us, and

because it reveals something distinctive about Fr. Donovan.

I recently had a long conversation with a Jesuit who has been at Boston College for longer years than he. In talking about Fr. Donovan's leadership of our academic programs in the institution, one word constantly repeated itself—one verb was constantly employed to characterize his activity. That word was Fr. Donovan's "encouragement." He encouraged students to go into new programs. He encouraged faculty to research and publish. He encouraged the creation of new academic programs at the undergraduate and graduate level. He encouraged all to the ideals of teaching. His mode of leadership was a mode of encouragement to the initiative and the resourcefulness of all of our people, an encouragement that brought to bear the resources of his own office in promoting the initiative and the imagination of other people.

Others have exercised academic leadership in other ways, but I believe that Fr. Donovan's exercise of leadership to encourage says something important about himself. It reveals his profound respect for the individuality of every man and woman and every young student whom he encounters. It reveals his respect for their liberty, for their imagination, for their resourcefulness. It reveals also the breadth of intelligence and of heart that are his own—his ability to appreciate broad ranges of ideas, and broad spectra of values, to support those that are worthwhile, to disregard those that are unproductive.

Fr. Donovan's style of leadership reveals also an innate sense of modesty—modesty that is confident of the powers of intelligence that are his, but recognizes those powers as gifts that have been given him, gifts to be used in service of others. Through his encouragement of the resourcefulness and initiative of all, I believe that Fr. Donovan, in 26 years, has done much to make Boston College a collegium—a colleagueship of men and women, employing their talents and their hearts' energies together in the creation of an educational institution. I would hope, Fr. Donovan, that our ceremonies today and our words today do not serve to encourage you so much as to confirm you in your awareness of all you have done for Boston College, and to confirm you in our deep affection and appreciation for you.

Charles F. Donovan, S.J. (1912–98; A&S '33), after securing his doctorate from Yale in 1948, returned to his alma mater and became the founding dean of the School of Education in 1952. As academic vice president (1961–68) and senior vice president and dean of faculties (1968–79), Fr. Donovan had a powerful influence on the University's academic advance. He guided the College's faculty development and its academic ambitions with brilliance, urbanity, and grace. He served as University historian from 1979 until his death in 1998.

Margaret A. Dwyer

May 17, 1998

*Hers was a faultless eye for the big picture and
for every element in the landscape.*

W ITH ONLY MOMENTS to introduce Peg Dwyer, I am
fortunate that universities, unlike any other institution in the
world, have a voice and a language of their own, to express
their admiration, their gratitude, and their love. In public
ceremony, a university can espouse a person as daughter or
son, worthy of the respected name "doctor," not because of
credit hours earned in class, but because of who they are in
the life of the University and in the lives of others.

Most of you in the audience tonight, trustees, spouses, the
president's inner circle, know Peg personally. For the thousands in the stadium tomorrow, there will be an eloquent
citation to sketch at least the outline of her meaning to Boston College. Among this gathering of friends, I would like
to share just one word of tribute from the perspective that is
uniquely mine.

Individual area vice presidents in universities—in academic affairs or in finance—make contributions to university life
that are readily understandable, that are clearly attributable
to them. Often it is their initiatives that the president is seen
to endorse, support, or to moderate—and occasionally veto.

In Peg's case, as vice president, executive assistant to the
president, and liaison to the Board of Trustees, it was too
often I who was credited with organizational skill, or good

judgment, or quality control, or thoughtfulness to the needs of the weak and of the strong, when the professional know-how and the judgment and the understanding really was Peg's. Hers was a faultless eye for the big picture and for every element in the landscape. Peg Dwyer's name belongs on every page of Boston College's bright history of the past 25 years.

Since 1960, her professional life has been divided between two Jesuit institutions of higher education, LeMoyne College and Boston College. Each is also her alma mater. The Board of Trustees of each institution has recognized the full measure of Peg's accomplishments and her ideals. As of tomorrow, both of the institutions she professionally served will have conferred on her an honorary doctoral degree, their highest expression of honor, of gratitude, and of love.

I am happy to present Peg Dwyer.

Margaret A. Dwyer (M.Ed. '56; LLD '98) returned to Boston College in January 1973 as executive assistant to the president. Dwyer was the first female vice president at Boston College (1973–97), serving as the liaison to the Board of Trustees and the person responsible for quality control of the operations and staff of the President's Office.

Frank B. Campanella

May 3, 1991

Frank's directness and honesty and avoidance of gamesmanship both in word and in deed conveyed an atmosphere of realism and of trustworthiness that healed divisions.

THERE WAS A time in my teaching days when I used to clock the speed of my memory in measuring the time it took to learn the names and faces of every new class of students of 50. My memory is still working effectively enough to recall 18 years ago approaching a young, prematurely white-haired faculty member at a cocktail party in Philomatheia Hall and asking whether he would be interested in becoming a candidate for the position of executive vice president that had been vacant for the past two years. Without a single moment of hesitation he said, "Yes, I think I would"—and a month or two later we had ourselves one of the country's finest executive vice presidents. Best of all, despite the extraordinary amount of time and energy he has put into his responsibilities, Frank does not have one more gray hair *today* than he had the day he began.

Obviously, I cannot begin to summarize Frank's accomplishments over the past 18 years, nor the range of abilities that he brought to them. One way to understand Frank's contribution to the College, however, is to go back 18 years ago and identify the three areas where I felt a special need for managerial assistance in the President's Office.

In 1973, Boston College had just completed the Hillside

dormitories and had undertaken the first major campus renovation of many that we were planning—that of Gasson Hall. The man who had been serving as campus planner since the early '60s was approaching retirement and failing in health. There was a great need within the ambit of the President's Office itself for a fund of experience and judgment to assist in the oversight of the comprehensive physical transformation of the campus we were about to undertake.

On the financial front, John Smith's first two years had stanched the flow of red ink of the early '70s and put systems in place so that it would now be possible to control our fiscal fortunes, and by mid-'73 we had devised a financial plan that assured us that we really had an institutional future. But great vulnerability remained, and there was an urgent need for a firm and sensitive hand in relating our fiscal resources to the burgeoning needs in every area of the University's operations.

The final need was perhaps best expressed in a comment of a senior officer from the University of Chicago who spent several days examining Boston College and in an exit visit told me, "Fr., this is not the largest university I have ever examined, but it is certainly one of the most complex." Given the complexity of the University, there was a critical need for an individual of judgment and dedication and loyalty with whom to share some of the day-to-day complexities of managing this large University.

Though there is no one monument or landmark that epitomizes Frank's contribution over the past 18 years, evidence of those contributions is all about us in the technology that facilitates your research, in the professionalism of the architects we recruited to create an O'Neill Library or in a Conte Forum or a renewed Fulton Hall; and no department chairman fills a vacancy or recaptures a faculty office or awards an additional graduate fellowship without Frank's fingerprints somewhere on the system or on the actual document employed.

This University, however, is no mere string of events, however successful, or of processes and systems, however efficient, or of buildings, however dramatic. There really is a spirit to Boston College that is one of its more valuable assets. Frank's role in the rebuilding and the enhancement of the spirit of Boston College has been one of the most important ways in which he has touched everyone. Like most American universities from 1967 to 1972, Boston College experienced the growth of distrust and suspicion between faculty and administration that threatened the capacity for effective decision making at every level of the University. Frank's directness and honesty and avoidance of gamesmanship both in word and in deed conveyed an atmosphere of realism and of trustworthiness that healed divisions. People will endure hardship and obstacles and even negative answers, provided they are dealt with honestly and provided they trust the source. Dr. Campanella is, if you will pardon the expression, refreshingly Frank, and his honesty and directness and professionalism and integrity have helped shape the spirit of the University.

I am sure it will not come as a surprise when I say that a major part of Frank's success as an executive lies in the fact that he remains an excellent teacher. There are lecturers who are capable of the grand, sweeping synthesis, but the truly effective teacher is above all analytical. He or she must be able to put himself in the mind of others and take apart complex problems, piece by piece, in orderly, methodic steps in order to put them all back together in an artistic whole that makes sense to other people.

Whether dealing with trustees, vice presidents, deans, or fellow faculty, Frank had the ability to disassemble the reasons behind the most complex of policy proposals or managerial decisions in order to assure that everyone was on the same page as the discussion continued.

I am sure that all of you, his colleagues on the faculty, and especially the students, take special joy in the fact that Frank is relinquishing his managerial role only to resume his highly effective role as a finance professor. For all that he has accomplished as executive vice president in the past 18 years, all of us say a heartfelt "thank-you" and a word of enthusiastic encouragement as you return to the classroom.

Frank Campanella served as executive vice president from 1973 to 1991, and from 1994 until 2001. In the intervening years, he returned to the Carroll School of Management faculty, but his successor remained in Campanella's former position until only January 1993. In September 1994, he reassumed the position of executive vice president and held the post for the next eight years. During his years as executive vice president, Frank was one of the key figures in the administration's centralized development of its physical expansion, its financial stability, and its professionalized management.

John R. Smith

May 29, 1991

*John is that rare individual who brought to Boston College
a business experience he could not have gained if
his entire life had been spent in academia.*

T HIS HAS BEEN a difficult year for celebrating and, at the same time, regretting transitions into retirement for Bill Flynn and for Frank Campanella and now for John Smith. Each has obviously stirred regrets as well as rekindled the powerful reasons for gratitude that all of us experience.

In my own case, sentiments toward John Smith are indeed unique. When I came to Boston in the summer of 1972 to interview for the position of president, the one University officer with whom I asked to speak was John. I had assiduously studied the financial statements for the previous years, and wanted to hear firsthand from the CFO his oral assessment of the challenging picture the certified financials presented.

The first University employee I met during those interviews was the young woman who was serving as the secretary to the search committee and whom I later appointed as my own secretary.

In my own case, those two early meetings flourished into not only a highly productive professional colleagueship, but into close friendship. If there is regret on my part in seeing John take retirement, and there is, it is tempered by the realization that he should feel unreservedly satisfied and proud with what he has accomplished.

Quite simply, John Smith has been three things to Boston College. In his earliest days, he meant survival for a nearly bankrupt institution. In all of his years, he has meant technical expertise in the creation of systems and controls that instilled total confidence in the financial management of the institution. And perhaps most importantly of all, John brought a type of financial imagination and creativity to his responsibilities that made it possible for the University to make the enormous strides we have made academically and physically and in our enviable spirit.

Without becoming too graphic, let me simply say that John in his early days did mean survival. In the years prior to his coming to Boston College in 1970, the University had run such substantial deficits that literally every reserve had been exhausted. The end result was that we were operating on precarious short-term lines of credit. One more year of significant deficit would have meant the pulling of credit lines and the University would have been beyond saving. In the months prior to my own arrival, and with the assistance of some very generous and dedicated directors, John had already begun to introduce the systems to reestablish control and allow leeway to begin planning for the future. John's real contribution to Boston College, however, is not limited to the narrowly financial area. Perhaps his greatest contribution was that he has a largeness of horizon to give him an interest in everything about the University that is beyond budgets and finance, and that stimulates him to see beyond dollar signs to the educational purposes they serve.

I believe that all of us recognize that for the past 25 years, Boston College has been in anything but a holding pattern: academically, in the residential life of our students, in our expanded and renewed physical plant. Progress in these areas has meant extraordinarily enriched educational service to our students and it has meant a spirit of progress and of pride that affects everything we do. John Smith was an integral, indeed indispensable, member of the team that made this possible. If we had relied on the traditional methods of financing our progress either through accumulated operating revenues or through philanthropic gifts, that progress could have never taken place. John devised, and Frank, John and I, over a period of months, critically shaped and criticized and reshaped a strategy that allowed us not only to maintain fiscal equilibrium, but to invest heavily in the future of the College without assuming obligations we could not wipe out in 24 hours. If John had only been interested in fiscal soundness and protection of assets and was not a creative partner with an indispensable role in making possible our academic and technological and physical advances, Boston College would have had a radically different, less exciting, indeed less exhilarating, story to tell for the past 20 years.

At the personal level, I am sure each of you have your own stories to tell about John. In my own case, and in that of our other vice presidents, they are stories of extraordinary loyalty to Boston College, of professionalism, of thorough trust and reliability; and they are stories of boundless, energizing, rapier-like humor. In my own decision making, those who know me best know that I always like alternatives and am never sure we are making the best choice unless we compare it with other possibilities. But nothing ever prepared me for John Smith's alternatives! The best thing about them is the fact that they are there in abundance. The worst thing about them is that after the decision is made, the alternatives keep on coming in greater abundance.

John is that rare individual who brought to Boston College a business experience he could not have gained if his entire life had been spent in academia. But he brought a personality that made his business background totally compatible with the needs that every academic institution has.

All of us, however eloquent, have difficulty putting into words all we mean. I always thought that John communicates on two levels: There is a literal meaning that is always conveyed in the words and sentences that he carefully puts together. But even when the subject is technical, there is always something deeper John wants to convey about his hopes and ambitions for Boston College, about the people with whom he lives and works.

I think all of us understand both of your communications, John, and they are the reason why we are grateful for your having been with us and hopeful that we will see much of you in the years ahead.

John R. Smith (1923–2004; DBA '91) was appointed financial vice president and treasurer during a financial crisis in 1970. He employed his brilliance and lengthy business experience until his retirement 21 years later to make Boston College a model of financial stability and innovation.

Kevin P. Duffy

May 9, 2000

*Kevin recognized in Boston College's aim of
educating the whole person, the unifying principle
that gives cohesion to the entire range of student services
that go to make up our program of education
outside the classroom.*

As we celebrate Kevin's 24 years of extraordinary accomplishment in the position of vice president for Student Affairs, I am happy to say that I had the good fortune of having been here from the very beginning. And, since we are celebrating 24 years, you should know that Kevin's initial appointment was not the result of a yearlong, nationwide search. Within days of announcing an important Capital Campaign in March 1976, our board had named Jim McIntyre, Kevin's predecessor, to become vice president for External Relations and manager of the campaign. But Student Affairs is so key an area in the educational mission of Boston College that it could not be left without strong leadership. Fortunately, that leadership was already on campus. That same day, Kevin Duffy became our acting vice president of Student Affairs, and six months later, was confirmed by the Board of Trustees as the full vice president. Twenty-four years later, I believe that we possess some of the most imaginative and responsible and therefore authentic forms of education outside the classroom, as exist in the private sector of higher education.

Kevin's position embraces the most diverse and heterogeneous sets of responsibilities of any vice president in the University. I am not going to try to enumerate the innovations he has brought to each of them: to our student residences and residential life; to counseling and health services; to standards of student conduct; in earlier days to athletics and to the huge galaxy of student activities that come under his purview.

In exercising all of this formidable array of responsibilities, however, Kevin brought the same three common characteristics to all he did. He brought a genuinely collegial style to his managerial position. He enlisted strong, qualified lieutenants, shared responsibility with them and molded them into a cohesive team where each gains strength from the other. Frank Campanella often remarked that one of our great strengths at Boston College lies in the capabilities of our midmanagers. Kevin is modest enough and self-confident enough and expert enough to have created and to have led just such a team.

Secondly, in every one of his diverse areas of responsibility, Kevin always set a standard of quality. Student needs were never overlooked or wished away; they were acknowledged honestly and met. He was infinitely patient in recommending every best detail in the construction of student apartments and the (still pending) student center.

But most importantly, Kevin recognized in Boston College's aim of educating the whole person, the unifying principle that gives cohesion to the entire range of student services that go to make up our program of education outside the classroom. Educating for maturity, for responsible freedom, providing attractive opportunities to assimilate values as well as to exercise initiative and leadership, these call for foresight and diplomacy and above all, a coherent understanding of the extraordinary potential of the human person. Kevin's own religious and humanistic and developmental vision of the human person—of what each student can be—provided the personal framework to carry out the educational mission of Boston College.

I would like to close with the few words that I wrote for the memory book that will be presented to Kevin in recollection of his 24 years as vice president for Student Affairs:

> If '68 to '72 were the years of greatest tumult in higher education and '72 to '76 saw the calming of the waters, from '76 onward took place the building of a new edifice to carry out the task of education outside the classroom. And what a handsome edifice it is at Boston College—the rival in imagination and effectiveness of our finest Gothic buildings. Through these 25 years, Kevin, you have brought your talent, your dedication, and your ideals to the programs that carry out much of the distinctive mission of Boston College. The College will remain in your debt—as will the countless men and women who came to maturity during your vice presidency.

Kevin P. Duffy served as Vice President for Student Affairs from 1976 to 2000. During that period he oversaw a doubling in the number of presidential students on campus and the transformation of student development programs for undergraduates. In 2000 he joined the School of Education faculty in the area of higher education administration.

John T. Driscoll

March 3, 1988

John has always been a man with alternatives,
a man whose talents and personal interests have always
kept open a dozen roads he could have followed.

T HROUGHOUT THE COURSE of this delightful evening, we have heard eloquent testimonials to John Driscoll's extraordinary accomplishments, and to the values that motivated those achievements. The Boston College I represent had the privilege of familiarity with John long before his career of public accomplishment, and now has the greater privilege of enjoying the wealth and professional experience and of personal stature that he has rededicated to the service of his alma mater.

For all our pride in former students, no college or university can lay claim to the accomplishments of its graduates. A student's gifts of mind and of character that stir a teacher's hopes and expectations, are also the source of his sincere humility. When blessed with a gifted student, an educator is like a parent. He stands a bit in wonder and in frank admiration in the presence of gifts he knows are not of his or her university's making.

I have been familiar with John Driscoll's gifts for the past 16 years—an association shorter than that of many in this room.

To me, what is most characteristic of John Driscoll is not his brilliant record of public accomplishment. It is rather the personal stamp and initiative that has marked everything John has done—marked everything he has become. Many men of high accomplishment are honest enough to admit that opportunity was so golden that it left them no choice. For all their abilities, they were in the right place at the right time.

Not so with John Driscoll. John has always been a man with alternatives, a man whose talents and personal interests have always kept open a dozen roads he could have followed, a dozen ways he could have pursued each chosen path. John's professional career and personal style were not the result of chance or circumstance or necessity. It was a career he deliberately chose from among many others, and a personal style deliberately chosen to mirror the values that were important in his life; faith and family and friendship and professional integrity and reverence for every man and woman he met.

Yet John knows that there is something more to his story. Christian marriage at its best means that you made none of those decisions alone. Jean chose among the alternatives with you and for you. In those choices, the two of you created a masterpiece of a career, a masterpiece of a life—which is the reason for the profound respect and admiration and love of everyone in this room. It is the reason for Boston College's immense pride in you as a graduate—and for our happiness that among your latest alternatives, you chose to come home to Boston College.

John T. Driscoll (A&S '49) served at various times as treasurer of the Commonwealth, longtime chairman of the Massachusetts Turnpike Authority, president of BC's Alumni Association, and from 1988–97 as vice president of Administration at Boston College.

William J. Flynn

May 10, 1991

*If Boston College possesses athletic programs that know
their place in a demanding academic setting, it is not because
standards have been imposed from beyond the institution itself, but
because one man has fully assimilated the academic and
cultural and religious aspirations of this University.*

Wᴇ ʜᴀᴠᴇ ᴊᴜsᴛ witnessed a brilliant illustration of the
truth that a picture is more powerful than a thousand words.
Indeed, in the video we have just witnessed, there is a span
of tangible accomplishments, of warm human feeling that
capture what Bill Flynn means to Boston College more eloquently than can words of mine.

Others on the platform have expressed the admiration of
Bill's friends and associates across the nation and among our
sister institutions. I speak as president of Boston College, and
as a friend.

Each of us, I am sure, has his own personal associations
with Bill—whether they were in building a building, or in
negotiating a schedule, or in cheering a victory, or in his hand
on the shoulder of an athlete after a painful loss. Many of my
own recollections of Bill have a geographic setting: standing
on the turf in the Cotton Bowl in Dallas and at the rink in
Colorado Springs, where we talked about the plans he had
shaped there for the future McHugh Forum. I see him at the
Sweet 16 in Houston and the hockey Final Four in Detroit, at
his Distinguished American Award at the National Football

Hall of Fame dinner in the Waldorf, at the midfield ceremonies in Dublin, and in Miami.

Just one brief anecdote about Miami: In my first year as president of Boston College I left a meeting in Washington to attend a football game in Miami that was crucial to what Bill saw as a very promising year. I had to leave at 6:30 in the morning after the game to get back to Washington, and Bill insisted that he take me to the plane. The game had been one of many thrillers that we disappointingly lost in the final 10 seconds. When Bill arrived at the hotel door at 5:30 the next morning, with Marie beside him in the car, he said that he was so upset at the opportunity lost that they had been driving the streets of south Florida all night. That early experience gave me some cameo understanding of this serene but intense, self-composed, but fiercely competitive person, self-reliant and in charge—provided he had Marie beside him, in victories or defeats.

In celebrating Bill Flynn's career, Boston College celebrates much of its own recent history. And yet, I am not going to redraw the story of his 34 years for you, nor attempt to enumerate the programs he created or the buildings that came and went and came again under his imaginative hand. And I attempt no such a portrayal of Bill's career for a very special reason. Some men take their identity from their jobs; they identify themselves so much with the responsibility and demands of their work that they derive their personal identity and much of their personal worth from what they do. Others give to their work the dignity and worth of their own characters. Over the past 34 years, the position of athletic director at Boston College has taken its identity from the person of Bill Flynn. In the eyes of students and faculty, of coaches and sports writers, of media persons and commissioners, the position of athletic director has taken on a dignity and respect and integrity that it has gained from the integrity of the person who has held it.

This is simply another way of saying that in his service as athletic director, Bill Flynn has been a superb representative of the whole complex of ideals that shape Boston College. Bill has indeed developed from Boston College and its students a superb program of highly competitive intercollegiate and recreational athletics; but Bill is a former mathematics teacher and understands the essentially academic mission of a university; Bill is a father who understands the importance of example in the developmental growth of young men and women who gain a sense of honesty and responsibility and of personal integrity from the people they admire. And Bill lives the religious ideals that are part of the formative character of this University.

From the perspective of the President's Office, I can only say that Bill Flynn was the ideal person to take responsibility for the extraordinarily complex demands that face the athletic director of a university such as ours. Throughout the past 19 years, I believe that there has been a perfect understanding between the two of us. Bill could be counted upon to exercise absolute fidelity in following any direction I wanted the University to pursue. On the other hand, when exercising his own very broad responsibilities, he was a man of inner strength and creativity and self-reliance to whom any of us entrust those responsibilities and know that they would be exercised with imagination, with fiscal shrewdness, and with the highest standards of integrity.

Yet, for all these abstract expressions of strength and self-reliance, Bill Flynn is a modest, indeed a humble man, whose perhaps most immediately visible characteristic is his friendliness and approachability to the thousands who know him well and the thousands who know him only by face and by name. One of the measures of Bill Flynn's contribution to Boston College is the people whom he enlisted to work with him as coaches, as professional assistants in the management and maintenance of the highly complex organization that he oversees. I am sure that to all of them, Bill has been not only their director but their friend.

Bill Flynn has been one of the national leaders in developing recreational and intramural sports programs as part of the developmental experience of college men and women. Indeed, he has stood in the leadership ranks in an area of higher education that has evolved dramatically during the period of his tenure, from a modest, if exciting adjunct of student life, to a billion-dollar focus of national interest. And in the process, intercollegiate athletics too often has found itself accused of having distorted the academic character of the institutions that harbor it; and from every side the call has risen for university presidents to take control of the NCAA so that the NCAA can regain control of intercollegiate athletics.

In my humble estimation, these stages of progression misunderstand the autonomous nature of every American university and the personal responsibility of each university president for the academic quality and institutional integrity of his or her university. One does not have to wait for the National Collegiate Athletic Association to establish and impose academic standards of achievement on our institutions. Indeed, if universities have to wait for the National Collegiate Athletic Association to ensure that academic standards will be observed, then whatever may be wrong with intercollegiate athletics is not confined to the athletic offices but extends elsewhere into the institutions.

If Boston College possesses athletic programs that know their place in a demanding academic setting, it is not because standards have been imposed from beyond the institution itself, but because one man has fully assimilated the academic and cultural and religious aspirations of this University and melded them with a program of recreational and intercollegiate sports that have contributed immeasurably to the life of the University and to the developmental growth of the young men and women who participate.

Standing at the pinnacle of his 34 years, Bill should be as proud as we of the identity and character that he has helped shape for Boston College.

And I am sure that I can speak for every president with whom he has served in saying that Boston College is immensely proud that it had some part in shaping the character and identity of this former student and student-athlete of Boston College, William J. Flynn.

William J. Flynn (1916–1997; A&S '39), a three-sport athlete as an undergraduate, served as athletic director from 1957–1990 and oversaw the growth to national prominence of the College's athletic facilities, of its recreational and varsity programs.

C. Alexander Peloquin

April 25, 1993

*If music expresses the culture of a people,
it also creates it. Dr. Peloquin has created one of the noblest
faces of Boston College's culture.*

H OW CAN ONE express appreciation, in a few brief moments, for 38 brilliant years of teaching and composing and conducting and inspiring? Only by realizing that I do not speak alone. The presence of each of you, especially the former members of the Glee Club and Chorale, is an eloquent voice to express our admiration and affection and gratitude to C. Alexander Peloquin.

All great institutions have their treasures. For 38 years, Dr. Peloquin has been one of the luminous treasures of Boston College. To the world and the Church, he has been an inspiring composer; to audiences throughout the world, a thrilling conductor; to all of us at Boston College, he has been a reverent and inspirational teacher whose appreciation for music enabled him not only to illumine minds but to lift hearts.

Truly great teachers don't teach out of books—they teach themselves. Every student who awaited the fall of his baton felt the inspiration of his professionalism, the refinement of his artistry, and the depth of his devotion all woven into this single life.

If music expresses the culture of a people, it also creates it. Dr. Peloquin has created one of the noblest faces of Boston College's culture.

The words, even of great teachers, inevitably fade. Music has the power to endure. Through his music, Alex will always be with every young man and woman he directed; he will always be a living part of this University.

All of us who have experienced the first half of the program are able to wish Alex what I know each of us would want for him—the realization that he chose to take his retirement while still at the very top of his game.

C. Alexander Peloquin (1919–1997) served as composer-in-residence and director of the University Chorale for 38 years. Dr. Peloquin expanded the early Men's Glee Club to the University Chorale that he directed at home and abroad through a full range of religious, classical, and popular music that enriched the educational experience of all who participated.

Alice E. Bourneuf

September 30, 1981

*Alice's world never threatened her, never cheated her,
never betrayed her—it rather captivated her, and made a
claim on her generous time and talents.*

LADIES AND GENTLEMEN, I am happy to welcome
you to the first annual Alice E. Bourneuf Lecture. I am even
more happy to join you in paying tribute to one of our most
distinguished former colleagues and most beloved friends.

Undergraduate student bodies are one of the most transitory of human communities. At Boston College, at least, our
entire undergraduate student body undergoes a total transformation every four years. When Dr. Peterson first spoke to
me about establishing this lecture series, he recognized the
unhappy possibility a few years hence of a student body totally
unaware of the powerful influence Dr. Alice Bourneuf had on
fashioning the ideals not only of our economics department,
but of the University itself. It is to assure Alice's continuing
presence then, that all of us are gathered here today.

I expect that the most significant presence any one of us
has among our friends and associates is perhaps our capacity to have them see the world somewhat differently because
they see it through our eyes, and to appreciate the world
somewhat differently because they appreciate it through our
hearts. I would hope that Alice's outlook on the world, and
Alice's unrelenting interest in all that happened in the world,
will always be with us.

Alice's world never threatened her, never cheated her, never betrayed her; rather, it captivated her, and made a claim on her generous time and talents, a claim that she was always happy in meeting. Alice loved activity; had the talent of a great teacher in being able to stir people out of any budding self-pity or surrendering of aspirations. In all she did, she was more considerate of others than she ever was of herself even in her illness.

It may seem unusual that I single out Alice's extraordinarily humane outlook on life since she was so distinguished in her own career in one of the most rigorous of intellectual disciplines. But Alice was both professional academic and large-hearted public servant. Her discipline gave her a methodic and penetrating view of one dimension of the world. And yet, she brought to all she did in the classroom, in university councils, and in friendly conversations, an outlook on the whole of reality that combined scientific objectivity with lasting loyalties, combined professional dedication with warm friendships and close family ties and with very deep religious convictions.

I consider it both a tribute to Alice and a tribute to the lasting friendship that Dr. Paul Samuelson had with her that he has joined us for this inaugural lecture.

Professor Samuelson could not speak to us at a more opportune time. He could provide no more fitting tribute to Alice than to bring to bear on matters of national policy and of urgent individual interest some of the result of his own very copious understanding. We are most happy to have you with us, Dr. Samuelson.

Alice Bourneuf (D.Sc '77) was the founding chair of the economics department and first woman to hold the position of tenured full professor in the College of Arts & Sciences. Alice brought her deeply humane values and the professional ideals of her rigorous discipline to influence not only the department she founded, but the entire University.

Peter Siragusa

October 26, 1980

*If you are going to rouse the
spirit of an institution, you have to speak its language.
And the language of the spirit is music.*

Twenty-five years ago, it was Fr. Frank Mackin, the assistant to the president, who had the good sense to telephone Peter and ask him if he would assist with our marching band. Peter inherited a small group of 22 people that he gradually grew to 80, many of whom are here this evening. And during the course of the decade of the '70s, they grew again to the century mark, and today stand at the grand number of 170 musicians and flag bearers and twirlers and managers. These young men and women are one of the great prides of Boston College.

Tonight is not the occasion to trace Peter's long love affair with music or even to list the public recognitions of his accomplishments. All of us here at Boston College are aware of the 10 WPIX trophies received at the New York City St. Patrick's Day Parade for the best collegiate unit in the line of march, and the similar distinctions at the city of Holyoke parade, and his spectacular contributions to the Boston 200th and now the Boston 250th celebrations. Peter, of course, would be the first to recognize that all of these were only possible because of the talent and dedication that so many of the students under his direction were able to devote to our band. As president of Boston College, I would like to speak for all of those who went before me, as well as in my own name, in saying that Boston College's debt of gratitude is absolutely inestimable.

Boston College, of course, is an amalgam of many ingredients. It has its buildings and courses and programs and tests and libraries and books and ideas. But key to Boston College is its spirit. And if you are going to rouse the spirit of an institution, you have to speak its language. And the language of the spirit is music. Peter has been able to teach that language to Boston College and to teach it to its students. Through the language of music, in turn, the College has been able to express its own aspirations and ideals, its vitality and buoyancy and freedom, its sense of courage and constancy and even reverence. In dealing with students, Peter has had the great gift of a teacher—to be able to inspire young people to give their very best and at the same time to be able to assure them that in giving their very best they receive much more in return. And that has been his great gift with the people who are here representing the band over 25 years.

Peter, in the name of all the presidents of Boston College that you have known, I certainly want to express our very sincere gratitude to you for all we owe to you. Thank you very much.

Peter Siragusa (1928–2003) brought the power and beauty of music to the life of Boston College as director of the Boston College Bands (1955–87). His enthusiasm and warmth added a personal dimension to the education of thousands of his "bandies."

Wayne A. Budd

October 6, 1989

*The Wayne Budd I know understands
power because he understands justice, not only within its technical
limits in law, but in its larger meaning of respecting
what is the moral due of every person.*

IT IS A distinct privilege to stand before you this evening. I am sure that everyone in our gathering has deep sentiments of admiration for our new United States Attorney—sentiments of friendship and sincere congratulations upon his past accomplishments, and of best wishes in his new responsibilities. I, happily, am one of the few who have the privilege of expressing my sentiments publicly.

It is a special source of pride to be able to speak on this happy occasion not merely as one of Wayne's friends but also as president of the University where Wayne received his undergraduate education. As each new class of young men and women arrives in September, I cannot help but think of them, not in the familiar surroundings of their student years, but against the background of the future contributions they will make to friends and family and to our larger society. It is a rare privilege for a university president to publicly express his pride and admiration for a former student in the presence of his friends.

There are many among us who can speak with more expert judgment than I of Wayne's professional accomplishments as an attorney. My familiarity with him is on a different canvas—through personal friendship and through some 10 years of close association as a member of Boston College's Board of Trustees. Through those 10 years, Boston College has had the benefit of Wayne's intense dedication and of his prudent judgment on matters as disparate as educational policy and intricate finance, the planning and creation of highly sophisticated buildings, and all the pressures and opportunities of life outside the classroom for 14,000 students.

Trusteeship of a university is precisely that—the holding of a public trust, a role analogous at least to the part Wayne Budd will play as United States Attorney for the district of Massachusetts. Perhaps it is a commentary on American life in the '80s that the position of U.S. Attorney carries the centrality and critical importance that it does. Given its importance in today's world, I am sure Wayne's new responsibilities are going to call for every bit as much wisdom and discernment as that of any judge, the ingenuity and creativity of an inventor, and the courage and persistence of a general commander. The Wayne Budd I know has those qualities, and one more. The role of U.S. Attorney unavoidably carries with it exceptional power—a power that is limited by justice and whose whole purpose is to serve justice. The Wayne Budd I know understands power because he understands justice, not only within its technical limits in law, but in its larger meaning of respecting what is the moral due of every person.

I suppose every one of us here this evening is, in a sense, a product of our own doing, a mixture of sensibilities received within our own families and from our upbringing and surroundings, that gives us a feel for facets of reality peculiar to our unique backgrounds. And we are products of the more global perspectives on the world that we have gained from education, from professional training and experience. Wayne Budd brings to his new position an amalgam of personal sensibilities and of understanding and of experience that this high office in Massachusetts has never before enjoyed. Those sensibilities and understanding will uniquely enrich the office. His appointment obviously looks backward to his own accomplishments, and it looks with promise to the future.

When Wayne Budd was a young undergraduate student majoring in economics at Boston College, he was chosen to speak for his centennial class of 1963, introducing Robert Frost, New England's most celebrated poet. Fr. Francis Sweeney of our English department still keeps a handsome picture of Wayne Budd and Robert Frost, each in tuxedos, that captured that evening. Fr. Sweeney told me that it is still a moving recollection for him to see Wayne Budd and the white-haired poet walking down the wide aisle, through the crowd that jammed Roberts Center standing in silence. In his address, Wayne thanked Robert Frost for coming so frequently to campus to take his poems out of the textbooks and make them live in his own voice. That evening, Mr. Frost read his best-known poem, "Stopping by Woods on a Snowy Evening":

> The woods are lovely, dark and deep,
> But I have promises to keep,
> And miles to go before I sleep,
> And miles to go before I sleep.

Robert Frost would be pleased to know that the handsome, articulate undergraduate who presented him to the great audience that night has gone so far and kept all his high promise.

Wayne A. Budd (A&S '67), a trustee of Boston College (1980–97), served as U.S. attorney in Massachusetts before his appointment by President George H.W. Bush as associate attorney general of the United States. In the private sector, he was group president of New England at Bell Atlantic before moving to senior executive vice president and general counsel of John Hancock Financial Services. In 2004, Mr. Budd rejoined Goodwin Procter as senior counsel in the firm's litigation department.

John M. Connors Jr.

May 16, 2002

*It is that type of creativity that has made Jack Connors
a Distinguished Bostonian.*

How does one introduce the best-known name in
Greater Boston? Over the past 30 years, Jack Connors has
won the reputation of a Distinguished Bostonian many times
over, among his family, the business community, his alma
mater, the health care professions, and legions of fortunate
and less fortunate men and women and children. And recently, even among newborns, who have come into the world
at the Mary Horrigan Connors Center for Women.

Tonight, we merely award the title.

Jack is one of the few people who not only founded a new,
successful company in his home city, he almost single-hand-
edly created a thriving new industry. He transformed the field
of advertising in Boston from that of a back-office suburb of
New York to that of a powerful competitor on the national
scene. Perhaps even more important to the social fabric of
Boston, Jack has committed the talents of the firm on a *pro
bono* basis to assist literally scores of charitable organizations
needing professional help. In the process, Jack created at Hill,
Holliday a culture of creativity and generous teamwork that
is a model within the advertising industry, and the reason
why no one ever really leaves the firm.

Two of Boston's greatest cultural legacies to the nation
lie in health care—and in higher education. In both, Jack

Connors is the city's single most authoritative lay voice. I like to think that, beginning in 1979 and continuing to this day, Jack gained his sea legs on not-for-profit boards at Boston College. Today, the boards of Brandeis and three other schools claim him as a director. Next year, for the second time, he will assume the role of Boston College's board chairman.

For Jack Connors, the key to business and to life is in, what he calls, relationships. After successfully chairing the board of Brigham and Women's hospital, it was Jack's ability to forge partnerships out of rivalries that made him the ideal person, in 1996, to become chairman of the board of the newly formed Partners Health Care System, and of Dana Farber/Partners CancerCare. While overseeing some of the world's most sophisticated medical research and practice, the position has given him an outlet for his own unique concern for the sick.

Jack deals with complex boards of directors the same way he deals with individual people. Jack never gives just his name to a board or to a good cause. When Jack is at the table, either in a boardroom or at a private lunch, you have his total attention. Whatever the issue, Jack is there with a willingness to take on the largest or the smallest part in giving a helping hand.

I've known Jack for 30 years. Whatever the issue, whether the hopes of a worthwhile institution or a troubled business or a sick child, I have never heard him say "no."

The only question I have entertained over these 30 years is how Jack has done it all. I have concluded that it is not just that he cares intensely or is boundlessly generous. A truly creative person has a unique personal vantage point, a perspective all his or her own that allows him to see the world in ways that you and I do not. It's a vantage point that never wears out or grows tired. And when combined with generosity and genuine care for people and worthwhile institutions, that type of creativity remakes the cities we live in.

It is that type of creativity that has made Jack Connors a Distinguished Bostonian.

Please honor us this evening, Jack, by accepting your justly deserved place in the academy of Distinguished Bostonians.

John M. Connors Jr. (SOM '63; DBA '07) has served as a trustee of Boston College (1979–2011), including two terms as chairman (1990–93, 2003–06). The founding chairman and CEO of Hill, Holliday, Connors, Cosmopulos, Connors has been a director and trustee of numerous business and educational institutions. Also the chairman of both Partners HealthCare System and of Dana Farber/Partners CancerCare, Connors is a businessman and philanthropist whose creativity and generosity have made him an asset to the entire Boston community.

Giles E. Mosher Jr.

September 8, 1997

*Giles is never happier than when he is doing
something for those who need him.*

I REALLY CANNOT RECALL whether my first meeting
with Giles Mosher was at an alumni gathering or a directors'
meeting at Boston College or in the company of our chief
financial officer meeting with our bank president when I arrived in Boston 25 years ago.

But in the course of those 25 years, and through the flowering of each of those relationships, it has become my privilege
to count Giles as one of my closest friends.

There are two of Giles's qualities that I would like to share
with you this evening—one in his professional role as banker; the other as family member and as friend.

The incident as banker allows me to say a public word of
thanks to Giles for the role he played at a critical period in
the life of Boston College. Some 25 years ago, the University was not in the healthy financial condition that it enjoys
today. Four years of successive operating deficits had left all
available reserves exhausted. The College was operating on
a sizable, multimillion-dollar revolving line of credit to pay
current bills and meet payrolls. September and January tu-
itions allowed us to pay down the loan, but the next month's
payroll made it active again. I am sure that one of Giles's
most memorable directors' meetings, prior to my arrival at
Boston College, was when he heard a fellow director suggest

the institution was unbankable.

I would like to be able to say, of course, that his shrewd banker's eye recognized the superb quality of the new management as a sure guarantee of future creditworthiness. But the fact is that in subsequent years, each of us has seen institutions with the same fiscal history collapse, when prudence required that banks reel in their lines.

Giles never wavered. Giles never once, in my first year, mentioned our precarious footing or displayed any uncertainty regarding the bank's support.

That was the reason why, some years later, when our financial crisis was fully behind us and I joined the board of the Bank of Boston, I told its chairman and CEO, Dick Hill, that I intended never to move the Boston College accounts from Giles's bank. Dick recognized a client's example of institutional loyalty, and I certainly recognized and recognize tonight the loyalty of a young bank president whose courage and whose judgment were tested and proven not only rock solid, but professionally sound.

One incident does not normally tell the story of a person's life and yet, among all of Giles's admirable qualities that have brought us here this evening, I believe that it is his unshakable sense of loyalty that is at the solid center of all the rest. What do we need most or look for most in a friend, or a father, or a bank president, or a husband, or a Catholic Christian, other than trustworthiness and dependability—what Gabriel Marcel called "creative fidelity": creative, because it is never wooden or passive or mechanical, but always initiating and sincere and shaped by the circumstances of the individual. I have seen enough of Giles's loyalty to realize that it is never blind or sentimental; it comes with the loving understanding of a father and the hardheaded judgment of a banker—but always with the generosity of a person who stands by those who need him.

And if I am any judge, the marvel of all of this is that Giles is never happier than when he is doing something for those who need him.

Giles, though you will no longer have to go through the torturous judgments of the banker, the long line of those of us who need you will continue to grow.

Giles E. Mosher (SOM '55), a trustee of Boston College (1972–78), has been president of BC's Alumni Association, president of Newton-Waltham Bank, BayBanks, and vice chairman of Fleet Bank. His good judgment and institutional support assisted Boston College through severe hardship into strength.

Thomas J. Flatley

December 3, 1986

> *I pay tribute not to what Tom has*
> *done, but to what he is.*

T HE MAN WHO founded Boston College was a Jesuit priest born in the town of Enniskillen in Northern Ireland in 1782. His name was John McElroy. The purpose of the College was largely to provide an education for the children of new arrivals from Ireland who were flowing into the city in such vast numbers upon his arrival in 1847.

If the College was successful in making its educational contribution to those sons of Irish immigrants, and in time, to children of many nationalities, it is a special privilege for me, some 140 years after Fr. McElroy first dreamed of Boston College, to pay tribute to another son of Ireland who has contributed so handsomely to the life of the University and to the life of this city. Tom's role as a trustee of Boston College has been altogether unique, insofar as his professional expertise as a builder and developer gave him a unique role in the vast physical expansion of libraries and residence halls and athletic facilities and classrooms and laboratories that have enhanced our educational strength over the past decade. Academically, Tom has also been a moving spirit in the valuable Irish studies program at Boston College, and is now initiating in dramatic ways programs that will encourage and assist students to learn the fine art of sharing their own gifts and talents with some of the neediest in society.

Nevertheless, I do not want to linger over what Tom has accomplished, even for Boston College, because in Tom's case, what he has done is only an imperfect mirror of what he is.

The advice given to speakers this evening was to frame our remarks within the experience of our special relationship with Tom. For a person who has all his life been a teacher and an educator dealing with young people whose most characteristic quality is growth into new fields and new avenues of accomplishment, I must confess that my perspective, even toward my own trustees, is unavoidably, at times, that of educator. And to the educator's eye, what repeatedly strikes me about Tom Flatley, beyond all he has done, is that he is a mature man still rapidly growing, one whose talent is so great that the accomplishments that have been are only the promise of what is still possible.

Because I pay tribute not to what Tom has done, but to what he is, my remarks are not so much those of praise, as they are of frank admiration—the admiration that teachers always experience when they come upon almost boundless talent. But because I pay tribute to talents that are sheer gifts to Tom—gifts from childhood family, from a mother walking through green fields, from his faith that gives eyes to see what others do not—I trust that my words will cause for Tom not embarrassment, but rather thankfulness for gifts received.

Where did Tom gain that sense of fierce independence that as a young man allowed him to take help from others only on condition that he knew he would pay back his creditor in full? Whence his sense of respect for the dignity of every person and for the value and worth of their work, whatever it might be? From where his recognition of the paramount importance of helping others? Where his humor? Where his enjoyment of sports and his absolute zest for life? And, for a man whose lifestyle of constant, ceaseless activity is the complete opposite of the contemplative, whence that vein of deep thought and of profound humane and religious sentiment that gives color and body to your accomplishments? Tom had a hand in shaping each of these elements of his character, but at their origin there is an unmistakable gift not of his fashioning.

Two weeks ago, in casual conversation, Tom gave me two brief vignettes—one of himself as a child in Ireland following his mother through a field; the second as a lonely young man on the streets of New York insisting that a friend take his watch as security for the modest financial help he had provided. One cannot explain talent, any more than one can take credit for causing it. But one can admire it, indeed, hold it in a certain respectful awe. If your mother were to speak tonight, Tom, I think she would have done what I tried to do—not praise your accomplishments, great as they are—but as parents always do, she would stand back, somewhat in respectful awe, knowing that even your remarkable gifts were not hers alone to give, but that she first stirred the creative hand of God that has ever been present in your life and, it is our prayer, will always be so.

Thomas J. Flatley, a trustee of Boston College (1978–2000), joined the Boston College board just as the College undertook its largest and most complex expansion of its physical facilities. Using his experience as one of the area's most respected developers, he oversaw the planning, construction, and total reconstruction of 21 major buildings—including the College's most prized Gothic treasures.

Samuel J. Gerson

March 7, 1991

*The outgoing responsiveness we honor in Sam
always has a human face with hopes and ambitions, with needs,
and at times, tears.*

A T T H E T I M E of Boston College's 100th anniversary in 1963, *Newsweek* magazine published a wonderful article on the transition the College had made "from a streetcar college of 22 students and a single red-brick building" to its newly distinguished status.

In the 30 years that have transpired since that centennial, we like to think that the upward movement in quality, as well as in magnitude, has continued. I recall the article this evening because *Newsweek* sought out two students who were not Catholics to gain their perspective on the University in its centennial year. Sophomore Alfred Wellburn, a Unitarian, said, "I tried to get into Harvard but I couldn't. I came here because it is the second-best school around and I don't regret my decision." *Newsweek* also quoted a second student, a senior: "The only thing about BC is that they're a little stricter here. You're allowed few cuts and you have to wear jackets and ties to class," said senior Samuel Gerson, president of the BC Band. Perhaps now we know the origin of Sam's lifelong interest in markets for jackets and ties.

Ladies and gentlemen, as the president of Boston College, I consider it a genuine privilege to be able to introduce tonight's recipient of the Torch of Liberty Award, a person who is an alumnus and trustee of Boston College, the son of a 1935 graduate of Boston College, Mr. Samuel J. Gerson.

I believe that all of us have gained some perspective from events of the past one or two decades, on what the true measures are of human accomplishment—the measures that merit our unambiguous admiration for a man or a woman.

The key measure is obviously not material success or a high profile on the public landscape. It is certainly captured, at least in part, by the single word that is the criterion for receiving the Torch of Liberty Award; that word is "responsibility." But, in making the award to Sam Gerson, I believe that we are doing more than honoring Sam; in Sam, we can perhaps see a completely new meaning of what this measure of human accomplishment really is.

I'm afraid that some of us associate the word "responsibility" with an impersonal and distant gravity of manner, perhaps a *drivenness* by some impersonal form of duty and, therefore, a certain woodenness or insensitivity to the finer and warmer and more human aspects of life.

But responsibility is really just the opposite; it is an outgoing responsiveness to the appealing claims that our world almost irresistibly makes upon us. It is the capacity to live beyond ourselves by being touched by the beauties and needs and hopes and aspirations of those around us. Responsiveness to those hopes and aspirations, to a degree, allows us to share in the destiny of someone other than ourselves.

In recent days, we have learned again that soldiers depend for their well-being upon comrades, as do children and parents, women and men, and co-workers in every business enterprise. Responsibility is simply recognition of that dependence and responding to it.

No single word can adequately capture a human person, but perhaps the one word I associate with Sam Gerson is "responsibility," in the sense I have just described, of unselfish, outgoing, spontaneous resonance to the needs and hopes, desires and aspirations, of those around him and his instantaneous responsiveness in taking a part in fulfilling them.

There are three large intersecting circles that make up Sam's life, the circle of business, the circle of family, and that ever-widening circle of community needs and aspirations to which Sam is so extraordinarily responsive.

Unquestionably, there is no circle of lives that Sam enjoys so fully as that of his family and perhaps no circle that is enriched more by his care and wonderful humor. But clearly, Sam's love for his family is not the area of responsiveness for which we are honoring Sam tonight. Within the business circle, the chronological and geographic lines of Sam's business career are easily traced, from executive trainee to vice president at Filene's, to president and CEO of The Denver in Colorado, to California as CEO of The Gap in 1979. In 1984, he became chairman and CEO of Filene's Basement where he currently remains, since 1989, however, in the added capacity of owner.

A career of this consistent leadership in demanding retail markets is convincing proof of responsiveness, not merely to the unrelenting claims of business obligations, but to the interests of clients and co-workers whose economic fortunes are intertwined with his own.

Responsiveness to need calls for courage and it calls for self-confidence to know that you can make a difference. And if it was a courageous act for one of Federated's most promising managers to make a personal bid to take the company private, the loyalty and admiration and affection of his fellow workers today reveal the human face of this demanding business enterprise.

Sam's corporate responsiveness, however, is not merely to his own business associates and employees. Perhaps the largest circle of responsibility is made up of that nearly endless array of persons and causes and organizations to whom Sam directs his personal resources and his corporate philanthropy. Boston College was almost forced to defer the kickoff of our current campaign because Sam, who was going to chair our corporate division, had not yet completed his service on the campaign of Newton-Wellesley Hospital. One of the chairpersons for tonight, Jack Connors, told me that there is no part of the human body for which Sam has not solicited a contribution to receive some type of medical treatment and care.

Beyond all humor, however, there is a distinctive theme to Sam's corporate responsiveness to the array of hopes and aspirations and needs of this community. All of us know the cultural worth of the many charitable organizations that enrich the Boston community. Sam's interests have an especially appealing face: the Boys and Girls Club of Boston, the Juvenile Diabetes Association; Project Bread, Rosie's Place, Shelter Incorporated, which provides care to the mentally disabled homeless.

The "corporate responsibility" that the Torch of Liberty Award recognizes can appear abstract, impersonal, loftily principled. The outgoing responsiveness we honor in Sam always has a human face with hopes and ambitions, toward needs, and at times, tears—tears that, through his corporate responsiveness, Sam helps wipe away.

This academic year, the Jesuit order—to which I belong, and whose members, over their long history, established Boston College and literally hundreds of other schools the world over, celebrates its 450th anniversary. The thrust of this large educational effort has indeed been advancement of learning—the enhancement of young minds, with new knowledge and new, deeper, more expansive understanding.

But the ultimate aspiration is that its graduates use their talents as men and women of accomplishment indeed—but as men and women for others.

It is for this reason that Boston College takes special pride that Sam Gerson calls Boston College his alma mater. Alma maters can indeed take pride, but in the last analysis we all realize that they cannot take credit. We are here this evening to acknowledge that the credit belongs to Sam and all of those whose ideals shape his life—Geri and the children, his own dear parents, and all of those who have been with him as friends on his journey.

Samuel J. Gerson (1942–2003; A&S '63), a trustee of Boston College (1986–95) and first trustee son of an alumnus father, was a highly respected and beloved leader in the Boston business community who brought to the board a wealth of business experience on both coasts and the warmth and loyalty of a devoted son.

William F. Connell

ST. MARY'S CHURCH—LYNN, MASSACHUSETTS

August 27, 2002

*Bill used to describe himself as "lucky," but what he
really meant, deep down, was that he realized all the good things
were gifts, not of his contriving.*

JESUS APPROACHED and began to walk along with them. However, they were restrained from recognizing him. He said to them, "What are you discussing as you go your way?" They halted in distress and one of them ... asked him "Are you the only [one] who does not know the things that went on [here] these past few days?" In recounting the event later, the disciples said, "Were not our hearts burning inside us as he talked to us on the road and explained the Scriptures to us ...." Then they recounted what had happened on the road and how they had come to know him in the breaking of bread (Luke 24:13–16, 28–35).

Like the disciples we have just read about, every one of us in the past several weeks has been halted in what we were about, distressed at the sudden and serious illness of our dear friend, Bill Connell. Surely during these confusing but mercifully shortened days, our hearts, like those of the disciples, burned within us as we tried to reconcile our understanding of Bill's sheer goodness and the suddenness of his loss. Early

Wednesday morning, God took Bill to Himself. Perhaps it is only this morning, in the Eucharistic breaking of the bread, that our hearts too will find new peace.

To Bill and Margot's children, Monica and Bill and Lisa and Terry and Courtenay and Timothy, and to Bill's sister and brother, Kathleen and Jackie, all of us here this morning extend our most sincere sympathy. And to Margot, Bill's loving and constant companion of almost 40 years, let our presence with you offer the consolation that we understand your grief and your loss, because we share them with you. But we also share with you a sense of gratitude for the life the two of you lived together, because that life has touched the lives of all of us.

A week ago today, Boston College conferred upon Bill its highest honor, the Ignatius Medal—named after the founder of the Jesuit order, and recognizing the distinctive perspective Ignatius brought to the living of a full Christian life. Ignatius realized that the highest forms of religious dedication should not be confined to monasteries, at arm's length from the powerful forces that were shaping culture. He encouraged men and women to find God in all things, in education and art, among people of substance and the poor, in the love of family, in leadership roles, and wherever the greater good could be accomplished. Far from there being a conflict between religious belief and high human accomplishment, that accomplishment can be, if we make it so, our means of serving God as well.

These brief words linking high human accomplishment and religious ideals captured for me the life of Bill Connell.

In a great symphony, each theme has a singular beauty all its own; and yet one theme pervades all the others and knits them together to lift the souls of all who hear it.

The themes of Bill's life were clear and constant: family, friends, business, his surrounding community—and pervading them all—his deep Christian faith and love and service to God. Each of these themes he played with extraordinary gifts of intelligence and wisdom and humor. But through every surface change in his life, Margot and the children, his friends, his business and businesses, his charity to everyone in need, these were the constants. And always in the foreground, enriching every aspect of the life he enjoyed so much, was his deepening familiarity with the Risen Lord, whom Bill recognized every morning in the breaking of the bread at the Eucharist.

Each of us here in the church this morning had a unique perspective on themes in Bill's life. But however different our perspectives were, the aura of integrity and thoughtfulness that surrounded him made Bill to each of us one and the same. Every new addition to the family or to his business responsibilities or to the larger community he welcomed without losing any of the commitments to things of value that had always been his. It was as though the strong roots from which he had grown into full manhood grew stronger themselves in providing nourishment and vitality to every new branching out of his life.

People who have reflected on the beginnings of Bill's life here in Lynn have remarked that Bill earned every success he achieved—that no one gratuitously gave him anything. Bill used to describe himself as "lucky," but what he really meant, deep down, was that he realized all the good things were gifts, not of his contriving. His beloved mother and father, Margot and each of the children, his education and each business opportunity that came his way, his intelligence and good sense, above all, his deep faith and the wisdom to make his faith and hope and love the motivation of all he did; all of these were gifts.

It was this unshakable conviction that everything was gift that made Bill such a modest man. Bill knew his strengths, but he knew those strengths were gifts, unmistakable signs that he had the love of his family, his friends, his teachers and business associates, and most of all, through his gift of faith, he had the certainty of God's love. And it was this realization of being loved by others that made him capable of so much kindness and love in return. Everyone could look to Bill with confidence, from a business leader needing advice to a youngster needing an education.

Being helpful was never a matter of obligation nor an imposition for Bill; it was simply a matter of being who he was. Bill's profound respect for himself, right down to his impeccable appearance, his sense of fairness and integrity, his largeness of heart, none of these seemed to be obligations imposed on him, they had become genuinely second nature to him; they were habits of the heart that called for no lengthy deliberation. They simply were Bill Connell.

Today's Mass of Christian burial, for all of us, brings with it an inescapable sense of loss, and yet it is this, the Mass of the Resurrection that most graphically expresses the meaning faith had in Bill's life. No matter how distracted Bill's schedule, he started each day as a charter member of what he called "the Dawn Patrol," by attending morning Mass. In celebrating the liturgy of the resurrection for a loved one, we realize, as Bill did, that the mystery of the passion and death and resurrection of Christ our Lord gives meaning to our own experience of life and of suffering and of death. However deep our sense of loss for a life too short for our love, we realize, in a new way, perhaps for the first time in a deeply personal way, that death is not final—that the Christ we and the disciples on the road encounter in the breaking of the bread is the Risen Christ, the Christ who triumphed over death. The death we experience, like the death Christ experienced for us, is only prelude to a risen life we share with Christ and with all those who die in His love.

It is so fitting that Bill's final Mass is here at St. Mary's, the church where his boyhood roots took shape. Only a short 10 days ago, Bill's lifelong devotion to the Blessed Mother took him and Margot and the six children to Lourdes and to Knock to seek God's miraculous intervention in reversing the dread illness that had enveloped him. Our own hearts and our prayers traveled with them on that flight. As Monsignor Garrity recalled at the beautiful vigil service last evening, Bill characteristically said that he wanted to go to Knock so that if there were a miracle, the Irish would get the credit.

In God's providence, a miracle did not take place. But Our Lady was, as always, attentive, for Bill went to God on the feast day of the Queenship of Mary.

And so it is with sadness, but with deep gratitude and thanksgiving, with admiration and with love, this lifelong son of Theresa and William Connell, this son of St. Mary's High School, this son of Boston College and of Harvard's Business School, this son of Boston's North Shore, and above all, this son of Holy Mother Church, in full confidence and trust, we commend our dear friend, Bill, to God, who surely loved him even more than we.

William F. Connell (1939–2001; SOM '59), a trustee of Boston College (1974–2001) and chairman (1981–84), was a philanthropist and conglomerate business executive before becoming founder, chairman and CEO of Connell Limited Partnership, an international manufacturer of metals and industrial equipment. He was the 10th recipient of the Ignatius Medal, and in 2003, the William F. Connell School of Nursing was renamed in his honor.

Patricia Coyle and Karen Noonan

GASSON HALL

January 25, 1989

We could not fail to love them.

"I BELIEVE IN *life*." These words are taken from the profession of faith of Christians.

My dear brothers and sisters:

There are times in life when silence is more eloquent than words, when the quiet testimony of our presence to each other is more expressive than the most carefully chosen language. These are times when listeners are too spent for words—when emotions run too deep to be carried in language.

Tonight is not a time for lengthy discourse. The quiet presence of each person in our gathering this evening carries a powerful message—a message to Tricia's and Karen's mother and father and to their beloved sisters—a message of understanding, though we know we cannot fully understand, a message of sincere sympathy and of genuine love.

Our presence to each other, on an evening only one week into the new term, speaks to each other a dozen messages of friendship and of loss, of happy memories and inability to understand. Mysteriously, the tragedy of loss makes us realize how closely bound in community we are—and how much our lives—in happiness and in sorrow depend on each other.

Amid all the diversity of messages conveyed in the silence of our voices—there is one common theme—we are here to celebrate the exuberant, joyous life that Tricia Coyle and Karen Noonan received as God's gift—a gift that could have been otherwise—and that they lived gratefully, joyously, imaginatively, lovingly, and generously—sharing their remarkable gifts abundantly with family members and fellow students—and with the pupils they enthusiastically taught and cared for both here in Lexington and South Boston, and in Vienna.

Our presence celebrates their fulsome lives—and says to all the world, standing shocked at their tragedy, that we could not fail to love them. And in that love I trust we find renewal of our Christian belief in life that we express each Sunday: "I believe in life—life now and life everlasting."

Our belief in the Risen Christ gives us assurance that at death life is changed, not ended. He is the pledge and exemplar of what life is for each of us. But in the mysterious quiet of this evening, I trust we have a new experience in our own lives of that belief.

Gabriel Marcel, the insightfully Christian French philosopher, said that if we truly love someone, we KNOW that they will live always. Through our love of Karen and Tricia, we know now that, through the greater love of their Father, they live lives transformed in the presence of the Risen Lord.

Patricia Coyle (1968–1998) and Karen Noonan (1967–1998) were two members of the 1990 class of the School of Education who spent a year of clinical teaching in Scotland and Switzerland. In returning to the College at Christmas, they lost their lives aboard Pan Am 103.

Charles F. Donovan, S.J.

July 21, 1998

He proved himself a pillar of good sense and of institutional loyalty when the entire landscape of higher education churned into divisive wars.

T HE WORLD is charged with the grandeur of God.
It will flame out, like shining from shook foil ...
    and for all this, nature is never spent; there lives the
dearest freshness deep down things;
    and though the last lights off the black west went oh,
morning, at the brown brink eastward, springs—
because the Holy Ghost over the bent
world broods with warm breast and with ah!
Bright wings.

These words are taken from a poem of Gerard Manley Hopkins, the Jesuit poet for whom Fr. Donovan had a life-long admiration.

On Friday morning, Fr. Charles F. Donovan closed the last chapter on his 70-year love story with his alma mater, Boston College, and with his Jesuit and lay colleagues, both women and men, to whom he gave so much inspiration and shared so much friendship.

In his 86th year, Fr. Donovan blessedly maintained to the very end his brilliant intelligence, his delightful, instantaneous wit, and his keen interest in every new development on campus. Over the last week, he had entered the hospital with a recurrent shortness of breath that signaled serious weakening of his heart. But by Thursday, he was almost ready to come home. About noon, the following day, his nurse and he had an untroubled conversation in which he told her to be on the lookout for his niece, Terry, who would be visiting shortly. In a matter of minutes, he was gone, silently, and we can be sure, peacefully, grateful to God and to each of you who are with us this morning, for having enriched his life.

I am sure I speak for all of my brother Jesuits this morning, in expressing my sincere sympathy to all of Fr.'s nieces and his nephew and their families, and in her absence to Sr. Marie Charles, his sister, whose advancing age prevents her from being with us. You are among friends of Fr. Donovan, who know the measure of your loss, because your names were often on his lips, and because we too know that mix of unabashed admiration and of love that his talents and warmth inspired.

Both by institute and by vow, Jesuits have always been a missionary order prepared to go wherever in the world their Superiors discern the greater good is to be accomplished. For Fr. Donovan, the greater good during his lifelong apostolate was uniquely to be found within the culture of his native New England and of Boston, the cultures that had so deeply formed his own refined sensibilities and his ideals. Fr. Donovan never lost his appreciation for the discipline of his Latin School education, for the humanistic breadth and communication skills he gained at Boston College or for the sophistication and research depth of his specialized field of higher education that he gained in his doctorate at Yale. All of Fr. Donovan's Jesuit formation in theology and in developing his own spiritual life took place within the exacting intellectual and religious aspirations characteristic of the New England Province of the Society of Jesus.

It was this discipline and humanistic breadth and sophisticated research interest and cultural familiarity and religious motivation and perspective that Fr. Donovan brought to the faculty of Boston College in 1948 and that he successively exercised as founding dean of the School of Education in 1951, as academic vice president and dean of faculties for the full 18 years between 1961 and 1979, and finally, for the past 19 years, as University historian.

During his 18 years as chief academic officer, Fr. Donovan was the architect of Boston College's dramatic maturation from an alliance of strong undergraduate schools to assume full university status. During the first 10 years alone of his academic vice presidency, he initiated 11 new doctoral programs of study and oversaw the appointment of over 400 new members of the faculty. But if he knew years of heady and optimistic expansion, he proved himself a pillar of good sense and of institutional loyalty when the entire landscape of higher education churned into divisive wars that dislocated the equilibrium of almost every university in the nation.

Fr. Donovan's academic leadership was perhaps best mirrored in the title that he always seemed to be most proud of. If asked to identify himself, he always cited his preferred title—not of vice president, but of dean of faculties. I always believed that the title gave voice to Fr. Donovan's chosen style of academic leadership, a style that, for all its power, was built upon the unique sense of colleagueship and of trust he had forged with his fellow deans, and upon his unfailing effort to engage faculty expertise in forming his own academic judgment.

I have kept to this day a file of copious memoranda and comments and reflections that Fr. Donovan sent to me during the first years of my own presidency. Their pages are filled with his brilliant intelligence, his engaging interest in every conceivable topic, his wisdom, his encouragement, his directness in expressing his judgment, his unswerving loyalty to team members with whom he might not agree. And if the University has advanced academically since Fr. Donovan relinquished his large administrative responsibilities, and it has, each of those advances have moved along the same course he helped plot; they are within the same large horizon that he envisioned for his alma mater.

As an officer of the University for some 30 years, Fr. Donovan was to me, quite simply, the consummate professional in his field; and he was the consummate Jesuit; and each was the explanation and secret of the other. For it was his religious vantage point as a Jesuit that let him see, with Hopkins, the world charged with the grandeur of God—flaming out, like shining from shook foil, so that his professionalism was his way of serving God—and God was not to be served by half measures or by anything less than the generous measure of his own enormous talents and abilities.

But what an unfinished symphony his life would have been, if he had not had the opportunity, these past 19 years, to shed the uniform of administrative responsibility and serve the communities of Boston College Jesuits, students, staff, faculty in a new, more personal way.

In Will Herberg's famous analysis (*Protestant-Catholic Jew: An Essay in American Religious Sociology*), he found that what children want to forget, grandchildren want to remember. In Fr. Donovan, suddenly the stones of Boston College and its long-still voices began to speak. And they spoke in the loving, understanding tones of a devoted son who knew not only the reality but the aspiration. His years as University historian provided a more accessible stage for all of us, students, faculty, staff, not merely to hear the story of Boston College told, but to know and love this refined, engaging man of God and man of the world, who made so much of the history he wrote.

When Fr. Donovan rode the streetcar to Boston College

as a freshman in 1929, a family home stood on the site of this church—a newly minted Bapst Library had just become the fourth Gothic building to crown the hilltop; and from the Tower Building he had an unobstructed view of Beacon Street and the reservoirs below.

In the intervening 69 years, that gifted freshman placed the creative touch of his extraordinary talents and of his desire to serve God on every feature of his alma mater's face. And he has left each of us a legacy of admiration and of love that we fortunately had the opportunity to return.

May he forever enjoy the presence of the Risen Christ.

Charles F. Donovan, S.J. (1912–1998; A&S '33), after securing his doctorate from Yale in 1948, returned to his alma mater and became the founding dean of the School of Education in 1952. As academic vice president (1961–1968) and senior vice president and dean of faculties (1968–1979), Fr. Donovan had a powerful influence on the University's academic advance. He guided the College's faculty development and its academic ambitions with brilliance, urbanity, and grace. He served as University historian from 1979 until his death in 1998.

Coach John "Snooks" Kelley

ST. IGNATIUS CHURCH—CHESTNUT HILL

April 14, 1986

*A great coach, a great educator, a towering person
among the spires of Boston College.*

Everyone in the church this morning is aware of
how deep a gap the loss of Coach Kelley will leave in his or
her own memories, in his or her own life. Quite clearly, that
loss leaves a commensurately large gap in the memory and
life of Boston College. Many thousands of former students
and faculty members have belonged to Boston College. John
Kelley was a part of the institution itself.

Since the towers on the Heights lured him to Boston College in 1924, those towers have stood as symbols to thousands
of people of the encouragement and growth and expansion of
talent and personality that education brings. But the true key
to education is successful encouragement. If John Kelley had
any great gift, it was his almost miraculous capability with
people, but especially with the young, to help them grow, to
help them reach, to encourage them to the point of inspiration, to use their gifts to the full. This gift made John Kelley
a great coach, a great educator, a towering person among the
spires of Boston College.

And he exercised that gift not with learned lectures or abstruse theory, but with the ring in his voice, and the beaming smile, and the strong hand on the shoulder, that none of us will ever forget. John was not content to teach the things he valued through his own eloquence. The pictures and emblems that made his office so fascinating (and that his dear family kept close to him during his final days) were not empty memories. They were graphic expressions of the intense loyalties that he lived to his students, to his College, to his family, and to God. It was as though his own voice was not eloquent enough. He wanted to show people graphically how much he believed in all of these.

Boston College will deeply feel the loss of its paradigm coach, John "Snooks" Kelley. But great as the loss will be, it is also the measure of the enormous strength that his presence and his great heart gave to Boston College, and this strength will forever be ours.

John Kelley (1908–1986; A&S '28) served as hockey coach from 1932–72, and if Boston College could be called a "hockey school," no one more powerfully influenced that character than John "Snooks" Kelley. His warmth, infectious enthusiasm, and love for people shaped the spirit of Boston College athletics and made him one of the winningest coaches in collegiate history.

Francis C. Mackin, S.J.

April 25, 2005

*Frank Mackin lived that mystery; he lived
that life in grand style, in the serene certainty of his faith.*

Even through the last declining days in the hospital, the same sparkle remained in Fr. Frank Mackin's eye, the same touch of humor flavored every comment. The first 80 years, he said, were wonderful, could not have been better. The second 80 had been, he said, another story. Family and physicians and brother Jesuits understood that he desired no further drastic measures to resist God's increasingly clear invitation home. The invitation was irreversibly written in the faltering beat of his heart. With artificial resistance no longer blocking his path, Frank peacefully and prayerfully, in the company of his Jesuit Superior, went to his reward.

Of the many members of the Boston College Jesuit community who have closed their careers at the University, I can think of few whose loss has been marked with more heartfelt sentiments of grief and of personal loss. Jesuits have neither spouse nor children, and yet there was a mutuality of love and affection between Frank and his copious family of brother and sister, of nieces and nephews and grandnieces and nephews that made each an integral part of the life of the other. Frank enjoyed a unique place in the sentiments of his fellow Jesuits. We respected him for his wisdom and judgment. We admired him for all he had accomplished for the Lord and for people. But for all his wisdom and accomplishment, Frank never lost his boyish gift to see the world's playful side and its humor. Whatever the occasion, Frank was fun to be with. The world Frank lived and brought to all of us was a world filled with the goodness of life; it was the faith-filled Christian world of belief in Easter. At the same time, therefore, that we celebrate the life of this extraordinary man, we Jesuits share the loss that family, and all who knew him at Fordham or Cranwell or Boston College or here at St. Ignatius experience this morning. And in a special way, we extend our heartfelt sympathy to his dear sister, Kathleen, and to each of Frank's beloved nieces and nephews.

I have had the good fortune of knowing Frank for some 35 years—first through our involvements at Fordham University, where Frank served as provost. Indeed, it was Frank who in a sense changed the course of my life, since it was he who brought me to Boston College. Throughout those 35 years, Frank was to me, and I am sure to all who knew him, a quintessential Jesuit. The overriding inspiration to Frank's life, and the source of its challenges came, as it does for every Jesuit, from the way of life in which he had chosen to serve God and his fellow man—as a member of the Society of Jesus.

In his wonderful book on early Jesuits, John O'Malley says that it is through what Jesuits did in their ministry that one can learn what Jesuits are, learn how they define themselves. And what the early Jesuits did arose, in turn, from the energies found in the Spiritual Exercises of their founder, St. Ignatius Loyola, and in the purposes and aspirations that he wrote into the Society of Jesus he founded.

The overriding commitment of the Jesuit was obviously to serve God our Lord in all he did. Not to do so, however, in the classic monastic way as a monk, finding God by separating himself from engagements with the world, but rather by using the full range of his gifts to strive to find God in all types of human endeavor. Endeavors to do what? Of all the reasons that St. Ignatius adduced for founding the Jesuit Order, like "the defense and propagation of the faith," or "the greater glory of God," or to effect "progress ... in Christian life," O'Malley points out that the expression that appears most frequently—almost on every page of Jesuit documentation is simply the intention "to help souls." And by "souls," Ignatius meant the whole person—by providing substance for the body and learning for the mind. That is why the list of ministries of the early Jesuits was so long, why it seemed to be almost without limits—ministries of Spiritual Exercises and administration of the sacraments and prayer, ministries in hospitals and prisons, ministries of scholarship and learning. The way of life Ignatius sketched for members of his religious order was a total fusion of a life of human accomplishments and a life of grace, a life fixed on God and a life fixed on the total development of the human family.

In an extraordinarily memorable reflection on his life delivered last year on the 50th anniversary of his ordination as a Jesuit, Frank traced the story of his own vocation back to a specific pattern of events in his boyhood. If, as you can imagine, the story he told was dotted with Frank's irrepressible humor, it was the simplicity and the sincerity with which he looked back upon his life that stood out in every syllable. For all of the versatility that marked Frank's life, the one theme that knit every phase of his life together was Frank's remarkable genius for being helpful to people—people young and old, the children he baptized and the young couples he married, men and women, brother Jesuits, and lay companions. In his first assignment as a priest, Fr. Mackin took a powerful hand in implementing then Jesuit President Michael P. Walsh's vision of a new Boston College, whose geographic reach would go far beyond New England and whose programs would fulfill its aspirations as a full-scale university. Through six years in the Berkshires as president of Cranwell, Frank had the singular opportunity of imaginatively developing the Jesuits' only residential school for young men during the most formative years of their lives. Then it was off to Fordham University where for 13 years as provost and vice president he brought the warmth and vitality of his personality to what would otherwise have been the impersonal process of managing the Lincoln Center and Tarrytown campuses. Few Jesuits have the opportunity and the responsibility of devoting all of their energies to the ministries of the word and of sacraments. After 13 years of administration at Fordham, Frank returned here to the parish where he was baptized to become the pastor of St. Ignatius Church. Six years later, as he reached 70 years of age, he wrote to his parishioners a full account of what had transpired during his tenure and the series of truly momentous events that had taken place: "But," he said, "it has been the celebration of the ordinary liturgies with you which have brought me the greatest joy. I shall always remember them. After 35 years in school and university administration, it was consoling just to be a priest again— to celebrate Mass, to hear confessions, to preach—to get to know and work with so many good and gentle people. I shall miss you." But that was not to be his last appointment. After a brief sabbatical, Frank willingly accepted the position of Jesuit moderator of the Alumni Association here at Boston College, where he had begun his administrative service over 40 years before. For three more years, he brought his boundless knowledge of local history and of people and the warmth and wisdom of his advice to the gatherings and deliberations of our alumni bodies.

In what Frank Mackin did, one can find what Frank Mackin was as a Jesuit. Spontaneously human, aware of his gifts and generous with them, appreciative of sports and politics and history and Irish lore, a wise counselor and firm decision maker and canny reader of human foibles, totally engaged with the people and trends and movements about him, roguishly capable of pointing up the humor in every situation—but through lifelong devotions to the Blessed Mother and the Sacred Heart and through regular, prayerful habits of meditation and contemplation, in all he did, unmistakably serving God as well under the standard of Christ.

It is not often enough recognized that the Spiritual Exercises of St. Ignatius, whose energies and motivation became so formative an influence in the way of life and spirituality of Jesuits, Ignatius originally wrote for the guidance of lay people—a spirituality aimed indeed at finding God, but finding God in and through the engagements and initiatives of daily human life. Such a way of life is necessarily a life of faith because the ability to see that one is serving God in and through the joys and struggles of human life is not always readily clear or transparent.

Throughout his life, Frank Mackin lived that mystery; he lived that life in grand style, in the serene certainty of his faith: committed first and foremost to serving God, but doing so through accomplishing the first purpose Ignatius had in founding his order, "by helping people."

In what Frank Mackin did, one can find not only what Frank was as a Jesuit; we can find what Frank and all of us can be as Christians.

Frank, with abundant thanksgiving to God for your life, we commend you confidently to the Lord under whose standard you served.

Francis C. Mackin, S.J. (1920–2005), a native of Newton Center, served successively as faculty member, dean, executive assistant to the president, trustee (1972–88), pastor of St. Ignatius Church, and finally Jesuit chaplain of the Alumni Association of Boston College.

Joseph Loscocco

June 14, 1984

*He worked to assure that
many hands, however different their remedy, would
have a part in stabilizing their uncertain but
beloved College.*

W E FREQUENTLY MEASURE the achievements of our
fellow people in the dedication they have shown their family, those with whom they work out their livelihood, their
church and the people they assist through organizations
whose mission is to be helpful to others.

As we say farewell to Joe Loscocco, it is fitting that we
gather with the members of his beloved family, those who
have worked with him over a lifetime, in this his Church.
And it is fitting that we assemble in the shadows of the towers of Boston College, the alma mater he served with great
dedication.

It is not a mark of strong established institutions that
they depend for their survival on any one person. Once
firmly established, they take on a strength and momen-
tum of their own which allows them to withstand most
ordinary changes in fortune. Yet even strong institutions
do suffer occasional crises and fevers of upheaval where
demands of leadership are critical and are, therefore, costly
to those who carry it.

During the lifetime of Joe Loscocco, Boston College suffered such a crisis. From 1968–1972, practically every college and university in the land underwent profound upheaval that was fostered by social and political and financial and even religious turmoil. At Boston College, the dedication of its friends was so deep that there were divisions even as to the prescription of remedies that would best serve the University's interests.

During this critical period, Joe Loscocco assumed two important positions of leadership in the fortunes of Boston College. He was elected president of the Boston College Alumni Association, and shortly thereafter accepted appointment as a member of the Board of Directors and very soon became its chairman.

These obligations coincided with one of the most intense periods of activity in his business career and at a time when his children needed a father's hand. And yet, Joe stood vigil, with a small band of Jesuits and of graduates of the College during the height of its fever and used his time and his energies to cool its ravages until a period of healing and revitalization could begin. Joe's demonstrations were never partisan or polemic or delivered in panic. With tireless patience, he worked to assure that many hands, however different their remedy, would have a part in stabilizing their uncertain but beloved College.

The fever passed, as fevers do, and Joe enjoyed the pleasure of serving as a member of the reorganized Board of Trustees to enjoy the fruits of his efforts.

Boston College is proud of its historic towers and of its ideals. It is also proud of those individuals who set the College in place and who sustained it during periods of crisis and of trial.

Because of Joe Loscocco's unique service during a critical period that affected all of higher education, I would like to express to his beloved family a tribute of profound gratitude and of sincere admiration for a contribution that will always remain part of the fabric of his alma mater.

Joseph Loscocco (A&S '43), a Boston business executive and trustee of Boston College (1972–77), served as both alumni president and chairman of the board of directors during the period of Boston College's most severe financial and social crises. Through lengthy hours of patient effort and diplomacy, Joe's contribution to the College's eventual survival was unparalleled.

Shannon Lowney

GASSON HALL

January 23, 1995

*This was a young woman whose talents opened avenues
in many directions but whose search for meaning in her life
always led in the same direction ... responding to ... the
needs of those most deprived in society.*

"Do not let your hearts be troubled. Have faith in God and faith in Christ, His Anointed One."

Let me begin by extending my most sincere sympathy to Shannon Lowney's beloved mother and father who are with us this evening, to her sister Meghan and brother Liam. I convey that sympathy not only in my own name and that of Boston College, but also in the name of all of her classmates from the Class of 1991. I welcome each of you back to your alma mater.

I am sure that for all of you the towering profile of this building has already been a prominent figure in your lives, both symbolically and in fact. In the late afternoon shadow of this tower on your very first day on campus, we gathered on the Bapst lawn with high hopes and expectancy for the years beginning; four years later, in the bright sunshine after Baccalaureate Mass the class celebrated with their parents on O'Neill Plaza the joy and achievement of graduation on the following day.

Tonight I am sure you turned your steps toward the tower building with sentiments far different from those of your student days. A few short weeks ago Shannon's young life was snuffed out in a hail of bullets. Those of you who knew her well and those who did not, lost more than a classmate who shared the same educational experiences as you in growing to adulthood. In those few chaotic moments that tragically struck one of your friends, your own life lost some of its own confident predictability.

It was for both of these reasons that I invited each of you to join me in celebrating this Liturgy of the Resurrection, both to commend her young life to God's understanding love and to reflect together on the breathtaking experience of loss that death of an extended family member brings into our lives.

Over the past several weeks I have spoken to a number of you, Shannon's classmates—to those who knew her well and those who had shared membership in the class but not close familiarity. It would be hard to think of Shannon knowingly doing wrong to another person. This was a young woman whose talents opened avenues in many directions but whose search for meaning in her life always led in the same direction: It was almost as though her own self-worth depended on responding to what she saw as the needs of those most deprived in society. This intensely passionate young woman steered her course straight at whatever waves of need she felt she could help calm. Less of a contemplative than a doer, Shannon's search took many routes but was by no means over. Her need to help that began so touchingly in the hours she spent with destitute children in Ecuador was turning her eyes, at the time of her death, to professional graduate training that would open up a complete spectrum of professional services she could channel to human needs.

For Shannon Lowney the engaging smile and spontaneous compassion and intense attention to those in need are suddenly over.

For those of us who have lost a child, a friend, a sister, her death would be no less a loss even if it came as a result of a natural process. But our ability to understand its causes would make it rational enough for us to accept it. The loss of a loved one to intended violence carries an element of the irrational that makes rational acceptance all but unthinkable.

One of the greatest French philosophers of this century drew the stimulus for some of his most illuminating insights from his own protracted experience of violent loss in war. From his painful experience of notifying families of the fallen of their loss, Gabriel Marcel realized that the loss of a loved one is a mysterious experience that we can never fully fathom but that overflows from the death of the loved one to touch our own lives and to throw them into uncertainty and deep questioning.

I am sure that such questions have been revolving in the minds of everyone close to Shannon over the past three weeks. The loss of her bright young life to cancer would have been painful to us in the extreme and yet its cause would have made it, with whatever degree of difficulty, somehow acceptable. Death of a loved one at the intentionally violent hand of another is, for all its commonplace, an outrage that discloses within the fabric of our own life and our own world an element of the deranged, an element of the irrational that defies understanding.

At 25, it actually seems possible to plan one's future—to control one's future; despite all we have learned from history, we expect that personal life is completely rational. The first unreasonable loss of a friend makes clear that we must find a way to accept in our lives what all reason would tell us is unacceptable.

And so we gather around this altar to profess our Christian faith that at the basis of life is not mere rationality but God's unbounded love. We celebrate together the Liturgy of the Resurrection, commemorating not only the events of

Christ's death and rising to new life, but also the consuming love for humankind that animated His sacrifice. We gather to commend Shannon Lowney to God's understanding love, asking Him to pardon any wrong she knowingly did in her short days in the assurance that God recognizes the intensity of the love that animated so much of her young life. And as it is to God's love that we commend Shannon, I would hope that our presence here this evening helps us understand anew that it is the unfailing love of God for us and the loving support of friends that make it possible to accept even tragedy.

Shannon Lowney (1969–94; A&S '91) was a young alumna whose participation in a service visit to Central America stimulated a dedication to those in need. Planning further graduate study, she lost her life in an irrational attack upon a women's clinic where she served as a receptionist.

James F. Stanton

TRINITY CHAPEL—BOSTON COLLEGE

April 2, 2005

There was an intensity and sincerity to all that Jim did that reflected indeed the clarity and sureness of his life of faith.

THOUGH JIM STANTON'S modesty would make him the first to deny it, Boston College's proud towers stand a little less tall against their sad sky this morning. Early this week, our generous good friend, God called back to himself.

For all of the 35 years I have known Jim Stanton, he always projected a picture of inexhaustible energy and strength. When I visited him at St. Elizabeth's in mid-January after he had suffered a mild stroke, Jim was already exercising his left hand to make sure that it would be at full strength for the opening of golf season. In God's providence, that was not to be. But the gesture itself communicated Jim's passionate zest for life.

I am sure that I speak for everyone in the congregation this morning in expressing my deepest sympathy to his dear wife, Helen, and their children, Jim Jr. and his wife Patricia; Bob and his wife Julie; Ned and his wife Sheila; to his daughter Ann and her husband Leonard; and to Jim's brother Vince; and his sister Claire. It is rare that one encounters family devotion to each other that runs so deep. Severing so close a bond of loyalty and devotion through death is a mystery of loss so deep, it is difficult for words to capture.

How altogether fitting that we are gathering for Jim's Mass

of the Resurrection, here on the campus of Boston College. The Stanton family has bonds to Boston College and to the Jesuit Community at the College that extend back almost a century. But even among remarkable parents and siblings, within the circle of an extraordinary family, Jim made a place for Boston College in his heart and in his life culturally, athletically, religiously, socially, that was altogether unique. The College welcomes the opportunity to celebrate with the family and with you the life of this beloved graduate and friend.

One short week ago, we celebrated the Easter season, in which Christians the world over profess their faith that, through His passion, death, and resurrection, Christ our Lord once and for all reestablished us in God's friendship, invested our daily lives with nobility and worth in God's eyes, and gave us assurance that even death cannot undo the good we have done; even its power to separate us from each other has been definitively broken. Each time we recite the ancient words of the creed, we reaffirm the message of Easter: "I believe in life"–in life hereafter to be sure, but also in an altogether new way, in life here and now.

As much as any person I know, Jim Stanton had a clear-eyed Christian belief in life—again, not just in life eternal, but in the goodness of life here and now. And that belief was the foundation for his outsized, intense appreciation for the goodness of all the people and the places, the joys and sadness, all the activities that made up his life. The panorama of photographs thoughtfully placed in the funeral home for visitors to review last night made it easy to visualize the intensity of Jim's appreciation for each of the episodes of his life: the happy teenager among brothers and sisters, confident young college class officer, willing Navy recruit, freshly minted husband, father, father, father; maturing years with family, classmates, par rounds and holes in one; and every step of the way Helen at his side to help make it possible. "*I believe in life.*" These photos were not just sunny tableaux; they are a quick glimpse of a life lived in the conviction of St. Ignatius Loyola that one need not abandon loved ones and friends to serve God. God is to be found and served in love of family and friends, in integrity in business, and in kindness to those in need.

For Jim, God's presence was woven into the fabric of all he did; indeed, it was God's presence that gave a special dimension of motive and a special level of nobility to all he did. I am sure that as only one of 12 children, Jim learned early to think of others, learned honesty and directness in recognizing the interests of others, and gained the ability to look beyond himself to recognize the claims that those he loved and the causes he admired had upon him. And throughout his life, Jim's response to those claims, either of family or friends or business clients or those who sought his help, was a response that was so spontaneous as to be almost second nature, if we did not know that those responses were intensely willed as his own.

I have just mentioned the words that capture what to me set Jim apart. Jim was not a man for half measures. There was an intensity and sincerity to all that Jim did that reflected indeed the clarity and sureness of his life of faith, but derived its energy from the unhesitating quality of his dedication and his love.

During the year celebrating the bicentennial of the United States, I made a simple presentation to Jim Stanton in recognition of the extraordinary ways in which he had furthered his alma mater with his time and talent and dedicated leadership. In that simple presentation, I expressed the College's gratitude not only that his family had been so much a part of Boston College, but that Jim had made Boston College so much a part of his own life and that of his family.

Helen and Vince and Claire and Ned and Jim and Bob and

Ann and all the grandchildren: Jim loved each of you intensely. All of us share your loss because it is our loss as well.

James F. Stanton (1921–2005; A&S '42) was a former alumni president and McKenney Award recipient. In addition to his career as an insurance executive, Mr. Stanton had a close lifelong relationship with the University.

David S. Nelson

ST. CECILIA'S CHURCH—BOSTON

October 28, 1998

David possessed a serene and unshakable sense of exactly
who he was—of having lifelong beliefs and convictions and values
that were at ground level religious.

Bishop murphy, Mr. Justice Breyer, distinguished
members of the state and federal bench, esteemed members
of the bar, J.D., friends all of Judge David Nelson and Mrs.
Enid Nelson:

I am sure that I speak for my fellow priests in the sanctuary, but in a very special way, for all of you in our gathering this morning, in expressing our sincerest sympathy to
J.D., not only on the loss of his brother David, but on the
incomparable loss of his dear mother. If there is a blessing in the extraordinary circumstance of their passing, it
is surely that Enid was spared the pain of seeing through
to its finish the loss of her third son. To David's nieces and
nephews, I trust that our admiration for your uncle and
grandmother will further confirm your pride in bearing
their family name.

For all of us who knew and loved David, today's is not a
loss that is sudden or new, but is really the deepening of that
mysterious loss that we suffered years ago when his engaging personality gradually went into eclipse. That eclipse Enid
and the family assimilated into their lives in uninterrupted
love and in prayerful faith that God was with them in David's

tragic illness as surely as He had been with them in the joyful gift of a son and brother.

A week ago Thursday, I visited David for the last time. The grasp of his hand was strong; his eyes were restless but without recognition. But when I gave Dave a very visible sign of blessing, his entire face broke into the unreserved smile that all of us knew so well. Whether Dave clearly recognized me I do not know; but I am altogether sure of his recognition of God's presence to him and that it was a presence comfortable and familiar to him from the faces of all those who had looked to him for help in years past.

David was a highly public figure. But throughout his distinguished professional and civic life, David remained the unmistakable son of his beloved mother and father. Even those friends who did not meet each of his parents personally could have recognized in David's all-pervasive sense of humor an art he had learned from his father, whose talent for easing the tension of union meetings was his irresistible, gentle humor. From his mother, Enid, David possessed a dignity and a grace and a generosity of heart that opened both of them to the experience of pain but made impossible the slightest hint of meanness or recrimination.

These qualities were the lifelong setting for the gleaming intelligence that David brought to the Latin School and to Boston College and to the Law School. And they were the qualities that directed his trained legal talents not only through the respected institutional channels of law and practice and of the State Court and Federal Bench, but wherever a generous eye saw a need for help. For David, the days were never long enough, even on his regime of eating one meal a day, to chair all the boards, to counsel all the agencies, to provide a listening ear and a helping hand to a student or to the son of a friend or any one of a score of agencies needing wisdom and encouragement.

And from each of those associations, there formed a circle of deep and lasting friendships, a train of women and men, black and white, youthful and mature, clergy and lay, wealthy and of modest means, who revered and loved and boundlessly enjoyed the company of this remarkable man.

Like many of you, over the past 25 years it was my privilege to come to know Judge Nelson not only as a fellow trustee and chairman of our board at Boston College, but also as a close friend—in professional gatherings of all sizes, on ski trips and social events, in peaceful religious services, in long conversations on jurisprudence and through serious board deliberations. David brought to every situation his profound sense of reverence and his boundless zest for life, a natural dignity and humor, his clear intelligence and uncanny sense for the feelings of people.

But underlying all those qualities, I believe that Dave possessed a special vantage point on life, a perspective uniquely his own. That vantage point, I believe, was the source of his quiet strength and the wellspring of the enormous contributions he made to his community and to each of us. That vantage point was a combination of two ingredients:

David possessed a serene and unshakable sense of exactly who he was—of having lifelong beliefs and convictions and values that were at ground level religious. For a man who was supremely nonjudgmental of others, David had his own inner compass whose direction he did not draw from others or impose on others. That compass was set by his inexhaustible faith. David not only believed that what he did for the least of his sisters and brothers, he did for Christ. He believed that helping other people, out of love for them and out of love for Christ, was what his life and his talent and training were all about.

As a result, there were simply no lengths to which David would not go to assist a person in need, to enrich the life of a friend. David was to me a living example of what Christian charity is meant to be.

Rather than summon up our own thinning memories of the vibrancy of David's sense of vocation to unabashed charity toward those around him, let me close with a transcript of words Judge Nelson delivered in response to an award he received 10 years ago:

> As for me … it is a distinction to have served on the State and Federal Bench. Judgeship … at least in concept is among the highest secular callings in our society … But I must admit, it is difficult for me to be fully satisfied, particularly in light of what was the prime vocation of my life. I speak of the years in which I was truly public … trusteeing social programs, and advocating for faceless people, and urging others to consider conciliation, and representing poor folks and troubled folks and bad folks needing to be good folks, and community institutions wanting in financial means to do their thing without overly bureaucratic interference—and teaching young folks—and doing all those "people things" that "big folks" sometimes could not or would not do.

With time and experience and growing expertise, it is true that David's vocation matured into less immediate, but all the more systemic, ways of accomplishing his "people things." But the vocation to enlightened charity remained the same.

Today he knows with his first and best teacher, his mother, the reward that whatever he did for the strong as well as for the weak, he also did for the love of God.

David S. Nelson (1933–98; A&S '57, LS '60, LLD '79), a renowned attorney, served successively as a Massachusetts and federal judge, trustee (1972–95), and chairman of the Board of Trustees (1984–87). A man of prodigious energy, wisdom, and generosity whose door was open to all in need, he was a powerful role model and influence on BC students as chairman of the board.

Michael P. Walsh, S.J.

ST. IGNATIUS CHURCH—CHESTNUT HILL

April 26, 1982

*It was this dedication to excellence that earned him the title of
"Founder of the Modern Boston College."*

IN JUSTIFYING HIS own ministry, St. Paul wrote to the
Corinthians:

> "Men should regard us as servants of Christ and
> administrators of the mysteries of God. The first
> requirement of an administrator is that he prove
> faithful."
>
> 1 COR. 4:1–2

Your Eminence, Cardinal Medeiros, your Excellencies
Archbishop McElaney and Bishop Hart, Mr. Ambassador,
Mr. Senate President Bulger, my fellow university and college
presidents, my fellow Jesuit and diocesan clergy, members of
the family and beloved friends of Fr. Walsh.

Above all other qualities, Fr. Michael Walsh was preemi-
nently faithful to the twin roles to which he dedicated his life.
He was, in the first place, a dedicated priest of the Society of
Jesus; he was also a highly talented and successful University
professor, trustee, president. Because he fused both roles in
his daily life, his University service was more than a noble
profession; it was a priestly apostolate to which he devoted
his energies for so many years.

Our liturgy this morning, which has an obvious element of
sadness at the loss of a close personal friend, but which also

renews for us the joy of the resurrection, provides those of us who admired and loved Fr. Walsh with the opportunity to pause for a few moments to acknowledge the imprint he made on our individual lives and on our burgeoning institutions.

The chronology of Fr. Walsh's life is a story familiar to most of you in attendance this morning. Born in South Boston in 1912, he entered the Society of Jesus in 1929 and was ordained to the priesthood at Weston College in 1941. A scientist by temperament and training, he earned a doctorate in biology at Fordham University in 1948 and was then appointed a professor of that discipline at Boston College. He remained at the Heights for 20 consecutive years; 10 in the laboratory and classroom, 10 as the president of the University.

No sooner had Fr. Walsh stepped away from the leadership of Boston College to renew his failing health, than the trustees of Fordham University prevailed upon him to assume its presidency in order to resolve, for Fordham, a financial crisis and the searing divisions that afflicted so many institutions of higher education at the close of the decade of the '60s. Four years later, with Fordham on a steady keel and the painful divisions within the academic community healed, Fr. Walsh tendered his resignation to a grateful and reluctant board and returned home to Boston.

The conclusion of his 14 years in a presidency, however, did not bring any form of retirement. It inaugurated, rather, the third phase of his apostolate in education. Freed from his administrative obligations, he turned the treasures of his rich experience to even broader use, by accepting invitations to trusteeships and consultancies at an ever-widening range of institutions.

For the past 10 years, he has been perhaps the most respected trustee, and certainly the most cherished and relied upon counselor in Catholic higher education. In his service on university boards, vice presidents quickly learned that homework was an indispensable preparation for the close questioning they could expect from Fr. Walsh. But when approached for counsel or advice, no matter how politically tangled the problem or how intellectually sophisticated, one had the certainty that Fr. Walsh understood exactly every dimension of the problem. And if the speaker needed more than an understanding listener to assist, Mike's solution invariably came in the form of a modest but oh so shrewd question—Did you ever think of arranging your budget—or your curriculum—or your financing, this way? During the very last week of his life, Fr. Walsh spent two days advising a college in New England, and two days at a college in New York, putting the final touches on important concerns at each institution.

If the past quarter of a century has seen his educational apostolate removed from the classroom, to managerial and then supervisory and consultative roles, those same years moved him from the stature of a regional to a fully national figure. A moving force in New England and national associations too numerous to mention, Fr. Walsh, through the decade of the '60s, became spokesman for Catholic higher education in the United States. With the national reputation he enjoyed came honors, recognition and increasing requests for assistance from those needing advice. Honorary degrees were conferred upon him and testimonials were tendered from a score of institutions attempting to speak their gratitude as much as their admiration.

On Fr. Walsh's 50th anniversary as a Jesuit three years ago, I had the privilege of joining the presidents of Georgetown and Fordham Universities, of Boston College High School and representatives of dozens of other schools that now bear the mark of his insight and his wisdom. On that evening, I suggested that of all of the institutions that depended upon Fr. Walsh, perhaps Boston College had the one clear distinction of being the institution that owed him the greatest debt.

At the time of his appointment to the presidency of Boston College, he had inherited an institution with strong academic foundations, with deep community roots and a rich religious tradition. But his vision went far beyond what had already been accomplished. During his 10 years as president, Boston College advanced to new heights in creative scholarship, in development of graduate programs, in the centralization of the various schools of the University in this locale where they could mutually benefit each other, and in the physical expansion necessary to accommodate his high ideals. In a long article, coincidentally written on this same date 19 years ago, *Time* magazine traced the personal drive that had made Boston College one of the nation's best Catholic universities to its 22nd president, Fr. Michael Walsh.

More than anything else, however, Fr. Walsh rekindled in Boston College his own unswerving dedication to excellence. In his judgment, the influence of a Catholic university could and should be measured first and foremost by its degree of excellence—excellence in faculty, excellence in teaching and scholarship, excellence in academic programs and in student talent and accomplishment. It was the accent on excellence that made his years at the Heights the birth of an exciting new era for the University. It was this dedication to excellence that earned him the title of "Founder of the Modern Boston College."

For the 35 years of his professional life, Fr. Walsh worked with and in and through imposing institutions. Some he nurtured to prosperity; some he rescued from disaster. But in leading institutions, Mike's unfailing humility never allowed their imposing characteristics or associations to lead, or mislead, him. Perhaps the most singular characteristic of his leadership was the unassuming modesty of his public as well as his private personality. His tastes were simple, his personal wants were few, and his lifestyle, by any standard, was religiously modest.

Each of us has privileged recollections that provide the key to our insight and our esteem and our affection for Fr. Walsh. I shall make no effort to attempt the impossible task of expressing the accumulated memories that are in the church this morning. For my own part, however, several elements in Fr. Walsh's personality help me understand his unique capacity for institutional leadership and his personal humility; his unfailing dedication to excellence, and his ability—without any trace of judgment—to accept every person for what he or she is; his towering figure at the forefront of a whole network of imposing cultural institutions; and the mild tone of his patient and persistently effective questions.

No single virtue, however extravagant in degree, unites these paradoxical accomplishments.

Perhaps the most distinguishing mark of Fr. Walsh was the fact that his humble and loving heart gave him an unerring eye for the difference between the important and the unimportant—between what was substance and what was mere show—between what was facade and what was bedrock. Perhaps St. Bonaventure captured some of the secret of Fr. Walsh in his simple expression:

"*Non inturatur in veritatem nisi per caritatem.*"

"It is only through *love* that you shall be able to see what is true."

In the following of his vocation for the past 53 years, Fr. Walsh has lived the rich tension of his Jesuit life. In his professional life as a scientist, administrator, counselor to the powerful, he was always able to see God present in every force he dealt with. In his priesthood, he was always the dedicated scientist, the thoroughgoing humanist, respectful of the integrity of our human culture because mindful with St. John that God so *loved* the world, that He gave for it His only Son.

This morning, my dear friends, in the beautiful liturgy of the resurrection, at which His Eminence our Cardinal

Medeiros, presides, we say a final, sad—but proud and grateful—farewell to our dear brother Michael Walsh. It is not really a final farewell. For not only does he live on in the monuments that surround us on this lovely campus, he lives in our hearts, and he lives on in a life of joy and glory with his Risen Lord and Our Lady for whom he had such great devotion.

Michael P. Walsh, S.J. (1912–82) served as BC's 22nd president (1958–68) after 10 years as chairman of biology and distinguished medical advisor from 1948–58. In expanding faculty, buildings, and academic programs, Fr. Walsh's 10 years as president raised the aspirations of Boston College to the quality of excellence befitting its University status.

John R. Smith

OUR LADY OF FATIMA CHURCH—SUDBURY,
MASSACHUSETTS

September 15, 2004

*John was able not only to help
heal the body of the University—but to add
lightness to its soul.*

W HEN I WAS considering becoming the president of
Boston College in 1972, there was only one member of the
administration I asked the search committee to see. It was
the chief financial officer, John R. Smith. In the wake of the
crises that shook all of higher education between 1968 and
1972, the College was known to have a whole host of serious problems: questions about the University's academic and
religious identity; disaffection of its alumni; mutual distrust
between older and younger. But one problem dominated all
the rest—the very real threat of financial insolvency. I had
studied the financial statements of the last three years carefully. My question for John was: "Can Boston College sur-
vive?" No Pollyanna John, he had neither a "yes" nor a "no"
answer. But he had concluded, as did I, that it was eminently
worth the try.

Just a week ago, a very different Boston College glowing
with health and promise and with the enthusiasm and vitality
of young people all about, began a new academic year. It was
surely divine providence that God chose that setting, that John
so loved and helped create, to call John back to Himself.

I know I speak for everyone in the congregation in extending my most sincere sympathy to his dear wife, Helen, to John's children, Margaret and Jack and Bob and Tom—to Dick and Yvonne—and to each of the grandchildren. John had an uncanny ability to appreciate people in their individuality, and he loved each of you very much. All of us here this morning share your loss.

I have learned from John that there are rewards to being both priest and colleague and friend. Helen asked me if I would speak today in a homily, but also for those who were close to John, in the form of a eulogy.

And indeed, I could not be faithful to John's own life if I were to try to separate his life as husband and father and friend and thoroughgoing professional financial executive from his life of faith in his relationship to God. To the tip of his fingers, John was a brilliant, insightful, imaginative, rigorously professional financial executive, and at the same time, he was an unmistakably good, religious person, kind and considerate, irrepressibly humorous, intuitively sympathetic to anyone with a problem. John was always modest about his gifts, and yet he could not miss recognizing how extraordinary those gifts were. But it was one of John's children who recognized that simply being technically best was not enough; John's deepest aspiration was to make sure that his extraordinary gifts have an influence beyond the merely professional—that they would be of help to others.

I personally believe it was this aspiration that helped bring John Smith to Boston College.

In 32 years of close association with John, I have always had the sense of John's being supremely at home at Boston College, a sense of his having found himself, in a way that he never experienced in the more one-dimensional world of business. It was this institution of higher education that gave full scope to John's rigorous ideals as a financial manager and his Christian aspiration to have a meaningful influence on others in their critical life choices.

The role that faith plays in any of our lives is as elusive to describe as it can be powerful and pervasive. John certainly never wore his faith on his sleeve in a way that would make anyone uncomfortable. There are two equally sure paths one can take in finding God as a Christian. One is to recognize that God is totally other than and outside of this world, as God truly is. It was this insight of faith that launched the monastic movement to leave home and family and commerce and statecraft to devote one's life to prayer and worship of God. But God is not only other than the world. As Christians, we believe that God entered the world in the person of Jesus Christ, and in so entering the world, in dying and rising for us, gave a new dignity and nobility to each of us and, if we so wish, to all of our undertakings. It is a Christian thing to leave the world with its cultural engagements and challenges in order to find God. And it is also Christian, in the words of St. Ignatius Loyola, to find God in all things. "Whatever you do" says St. Paul, "do it in the name of our Lord, Jesus Christ." "Whatever you did for one of these least brothers of mine, you did for me." What turns professional accomplishment into religious meaning is motivation of faith.

The great Jesuit archaeologist of the last century, Teilhard de Chardin, whose scholarship involved digging through the dust of antiquity, graphically yet simply expressed this Christian vision of human life in saying that God is found not only in withdrawal from the world in prayer or meditation. God is "at the tip of my pen, my spade, my brush ... of my heart and of my thought. By pressing the stroke, the line ... on which I am engaged, to its ultimate natural finish, I shall arrive at the ultimate aim toward which my innermost will tends." If the city of God could be built through the scholar's pen, and that is the basic Christian insight and belief that underlies Boston College and every Jesuit university that aspires to professional excellence, that same city of God is equally to be built by a mother's love of a child or the sophisticated devising of a loan program to assist parents in educating their children or in conceiving a new technique for financing a university's complex capital needs.

John's faith and his prayer gave a religious dimension to his professional work; his work gave visible substance to his faith.

But while John helped the College become professionally businesslike, he never saw the College as a business. John's horizon was always large enough, and he was always modest enough, to recognize the primacy of the educational and religious mission of the College.

For that reason, John was able not only to help heal the body of the University—but to add lightness to its soul.

John managed all of his professional accomplishments with a modesty and a rapier-like sense of humor and a passionate interest in every facet of our complex university that gave sparkle to every team meeting and to every conversation in which he engaged. John truly was an original, and I am sure that that originality enlivened the spirit of the University, it enlivened also the spirit of each of us who worked with him.

The University's endowment is meant to last in perpetuity. John Smith left an imprint on Boston College, and through the College, on incalculable numbers of students and their families, that will endure as long as its soaring granite towers.

Best of all, who of us can doubt that God understood this wonderful, immensely kind, tough-minded, sensitive, practical, gracious man even more than we, and will enjoy his company as did we.

John R. Smith (1923–2004, DBA '91) was appointed financial vice president and treasurer during a financial crisis in 1971. He employed his brilliance and lengthy business experience until his retirement 21 years later to make Boston College a model of financial stability and innovation.

Einar Paul Robsham

February 26, 2004

This was not a man who shared his troubles or his sadness;
Paul always shared his enjoyment of life.

Twenty short years ago, I suggested to Paul and Joyce that we have a memorial service for their son in this chapel. In his typically modest way, Paul remarked that there were too few of his friends to attend the service. I am happy to welcome all of you to this chapel at Boston College to celebrate Paul's life and to express our affection and our sincere prayers to God for him.

Shortly after Thanksgiving, Paul and Joyce again this year, as they have in most recent winters, made the trip to Florida. Unfortunately, in the two months that they were there, Paul's heart, which had progressively troubled him in recent years, proved to be too weak to enjoy the fresh air and activity that all of us thought would be beneficial to him. As weeks went on, it became clear that they would have to return to Massachusetts General Hospital. The weakness of Paul's heart, however, was irreversible. Last Sunday, peacefully, and mercifully without pain, Paul went to the Lord.

I am sure I speak for everyone in the congregation this morning in expressing our deepest sympathy to Paul's sister, Lorraine, to his nieces and to his secretary, Pat Davis, and in a very special way, to his dear wife, Joyce. In the 30 years I have known Paul and Joyce, their dedication to each other has been altogether complete. Bonds of love that have lasted all one's life are hard to relinquish; and yet the depth of her loss, that we share, is itself the measure of how much we admired and respected Paul—and how grateful we are for Paul's life and for the opportunity we had to share it.

But for all of our inescapable sense of loss, we cannot help but be grateful for Paul and with him for the completeness of life and the fullness of life he enjoyed at God's hands. Certainly, Paul would have been the first to ask why he was so abundantly blessed with happiness when life so easily could have been otherwise. And in his quiet modesty, Paul would have been the first to recognize that his gifts were not of his making but were rather a reason for gratitude to God.

Except for his years as an army officer in Korea, Paul spent his entire life here in the Commonwealth—his boyhood and high school in Brighton, where he and Joyce first became friends, and after the War, his early career as a builder—a career that expanded and grew throughout the entire western suburban area. The mark of Paul's building career, however, was not just the extraordinary volume of communities he established, but the quality and care that won him recognition from a whole litany of civic and religious organizations— indeed, from *Life* and *Fortune* magazines. The wisdom and experience Paul gained in business made him a coveted policy advisor and a valuable board member at the University of Massachusetts, at Belmont Hill School Corporation, and, as I can testify, for over a decade at Boston College. That same wisdom and experience Paul shared in an ever-widening circle of hospitals and guidance centers and Catholic charities agencies and civic boards of almost every description.

Paul's lifelong involvement in support of children through the Boy Scouts of America was an indicator of his deep and lasting commitment to young people. From Cub Scout himself as a child to president of the Algonquin Council to "Man of the Year" as an adult in 1980, Paul not only honored the children's annual events with his support, he unfailingly honored them with his presence. Yesterday, the very first group of mourners who came to pay their respects to Paul and extend their sympathy to Joyce was the entire Wayland hockey team that Paul had supported for years. For anyone who knew the Robsham family, it was clear that Paul and Joyce's lifelong dedication to young people arose from their boundless devotion to their only son, Paul Jr. Yesterday as well, a Belmont Hill faculty member embarrassed Joyce by identifying Paul and her as the premier parents of all the students he had taught. Paul Jr.'s sudden, tragic death as a college freshman was a sorrow that forever marked not one but three lives.

I have had the good fortune to be a friend of Paul and Joyce for a quarter century. Perhaps the only time that Paul really worked at the bidding of others was during his years as an officer in Korea. For the rest of his life, Paul drew his own map. He was an initiator, an imaginative, creative builder who established his own company and expanded it dramatically to provide many of the homes and residential communities and apartment complexes in Massachusetts. Paul had the highest principles of personal honesty and integrity, but he never used the standards he applied to himself to critically measure other people. Paul was remarkably self-reliant, and for a man who had experienced both hardship and success in his life, Paul was a total realist. He was able to recognize and appreciate good things in life, appreciate good friends, and able to accept setbacks and sorrows without complaint and without self-pity. But if Paul had his share of disappointment, it only served to heighten all the more his love for life. This was not a man who shared his troubles or his sadness; Paul always shared his enjoyment of life—whether it was a closely contested golf match or the performance of a prize horse, or simply the sharing of a meal or a conversation with good friends.

To say that Paul was uncritical of others is to say more positively that there was an unmistakable band of sincere Christian kindness toward others that ran through his entire life. Paul was always willing to be of help. Indeed, in reading today's Gospel passage, it was almost like reading the story of Paul's life, "I was hungry and you gave me food, I was thirsty and you gave me drink, a stranger and you welcomed me, naked and you clothed me, ill and you cared for me, in prison and you visited me." Perhaps the most constant object of Paul's helpfulness and his charity were young people— in their scouting and hockey leagues, in their activities at U. Mass Amherst and Belmont Hill and Boston College. But his kindness was not limited to the young. His older priest friends, he followed in their retirement with regular, thoughtful invitations to assure them they were remembered.

But most of all, Paul's love was directed within the family as father and husband. Especially after the loss of Paul Jr., Paul and Joyce completely refocused the energies of their wide-ranging business and social interests to strengthen each other in their mutual sorrow.

For a man of extraordinary accomplishment and charity, Paul was the least ostentatious of men. Paul did not wear his religious sentiments on his sleeve, but those sentiments were deep and real. Among all the miraculous humanitarian goals being achieved at MGH, Paul used to talk to me about the human support that the chapel at Mass. General provided to families. Those sentiments showed themselves in his choice of friends and in where he spent his energies and his resources. They underlay his unshakable integrity in business and his thoughtfulness to young people and those in need. Born of an Irish mother and a Norwegian father, it was my privilege to confer on Paul the last rites of the Church during his illness this week.

I am sure that Paul has already heard Christ's words from today's Gospel: "Amen I say to you, whatever you did for one of these least brothers of mine, you did for me."

E. Paul Robsham (1929–2004; M.Ed. '83) was a philanthropist and prominent real estate developer in eastern Massachusetts. A trustee of Boston College (1985–93), he was also the parent, with Joyce, of E. Paul Robsham Jr., after whom the theater is named.

John A. Dinneen, S.J.

ST. IGNATIUS CHURCH—CHESTNUT HILL

January 16, 2003

Where there was doubt and suspicion,
Jack's outgoing personality immediately
inspired trust.

I T   I S   I N D E E D a privilege for me to express a few words of admiration and of respect for the life of Jack Dinneen, both in my own name and especially on behalf of Boston College.

Jack's work as a Jesuit and my own paralleled each other in remarkable ways. Before we were ordained, Jack and I both taught philosophy at St. Peter's College in New Jersey; we both traveled on the same ship to Europe in 1957; both gained our doctorates at the University of Louvain with large doses of our training at Oxford; both returned to teach philosophy at Le Moyne College; both successively became academic dean and vice president at Le Moyne. And after a few relatively brief assignments in New York as rector of the Jesuit Seminary and with the Department of Health, Education and Welfare in Washington, in 1979, Jack came to Boston College as our University chaplain. And in the course of those years, I must confess that both of us had the opportunity to do considerable damage to the fairways on the same golf courses here and elsewhere.

I am sure that everyone here has his or her own individual story of how Jack's friendship and intelligence and advice and humor and encouragement touched your lives. But I would like to say a word of gratitude for his contribution to the University as a whole. As those of you who were here will recall, Boston College in the late '70s was not quite the confident, energetically positive institution it is today. With almost every other institution of higher education, Boston College was still emerging from one of the most difficult periods in history—difficult because the sense of community that is the bedrock of the entire process of education had been badly shaken. Even at the end of the '70s, there remained unmistakable traces on every campus of division and of uncertainty and distrust.

Arriving as both a member of the philosophy department and head of the University chaplaincy, Jack was the perfect person to help restore energy to a renewed sense of community. Jack's entire outlook on life was so thoroughly positive and cooperative and constructive that divisions imperceptibly healed and new confidence showed its face. Where there was hesitation and uncertainty, Jack provided confidence; where there was doubt and suspicion, Jack's outgoing personality immediately inspired trust.

But it was not just because Jack had a voice in many worlds—from faculty and campus ministry to student activities to Jesuit Community—that Jack had so nourishing an influence at Boston College. It was because he brought the exact, selfsame outlook to everything he did—an outlook that respected the goodness and beauty and intrinsic worth of all he met and all he did . This outlook he gained in prayer from the *Spiritual Exercises* of Ignatius Loyola, the capacity of finding God in all things.

Spiritual writers say that this capacity to see God in all things is the key to Jesuit spirituality. It is the reason why Jesuit life, like that of lay colleagues, does not require the seclusion of a monastery nor the cowl of religious garb nor disengagement from efforts to advance the welfare of the human family. It is nonetheless a religious life in service to God, because God can be encountered and served in each.

Today, one of Boston College's rightful prides is its powerful sense of community. This evening, I would like to acknowledge with great gratitude Fr. Jack Dinneen's unique contribution to the strength of that community, and suggest that all of those of us who knew and admired Jack as a friend could find no better way of honoring him than to recognize the blessing he was to each of us and attempt to find, as he did, in our work as a University community and therefore in each other, the face of God Himself.

John A. Dinneen, S.J. (1929–2003) served as University chaplain at Boston College (1976–88) after many years as a philosophy professor, academic dean, and trustee at other universities. As chaplain, Fr. Dinneen initiated the Martin Luther King Scholarship Committee and the Appalachia Volunteer program. From 1976 until his death, he was a member of the philosophy department.

Michael J. Mansfield

FORT MEAD CHAPEL—ARLINGTON, VIRGINIA

October 10, 2001

Those who worked closest with
Ambassador Mansfield never heard
a word spoken in anger.

LAST WEEK, ONE of America's most admired and respected public servants went to God after 98 productive
years, 44 of them in direct service of his nation. The toll of
his years and of his illness had indeed become visible, but by
contrast it had only succeeded in enhancing this great man's
clarity of mind, his appreciation for life and the peace and
perspective faith gave him in living his own life. On this Friday past, the Lord Himself came to share with Senator Mike
Mansfield his own risen life.

The University I served as president for two and one-half
decades, Boston College, has had a long-standing admiration for Senator Mansfield, honoring him most recently with
its Distinguished Citizenship Award bearing the name of
the senator's close friend and colleague, Speaker Thomas P.
O'Neill.

I am sure that I speak, not only for my University, but for
everyone in this assembly this morning, in expressing deepest sympathy to the senator's daughter, Ann Mansfield, to his
granddaughter, Caroline, and to the other members of the
family. Bonds of love that have lasted all one's life are hard
to relinquish, and yet loss itself is the measure of how much

all America has to be thankful for in his life and for the opp-ortunities you had to share in it.

I have always believed that it is the Mass of Christian Buri-al that most graphically expresses the fundamental mean-ing that faith brings to the experience of death. So often, our faith can seem confined to benign ritual without engaging our deeper selves. But as we have all too sadly learned in re-cent days, in celebrating the liturgy of the resurrection for one we have deeply admired and come to love, we realize in a personal way that if the mystery of the passion and death of Christ our Lord gives meaning to our own sadness, it is faith in his resurrection that gives Christian meaning to the ending of earthly existence. We realize in a new way, perhaps for the first time in a deeply personal way, that death is not final—that death we experience like the death Christ expe-rienced for us, is only prelude to a risen life we share with Christ and with all those who died in His love.

Indeed, the Mass celebrating the life of an elderly person reaffirms in a special way the profound meaning of our faith. For however deep our love for a lifelong family member or our respect and admiration for a longtime friend, in an older person there is a sense of completeness of life and of desti-ny realized that clothes sadness with gratitude and sincere thanksgiving for his generous gifts.

Certainly in God's providence, this son of humble immi-grant parents enjoyed completeness of life, not only in what he experienced, but even more in what he contributed to the world. It is not my place to chronicle events in the 44 years of his distinguished public service to the nation. Statecraft and diplomacy, however, certainly rank among the noblest of hu-man callings. It is through statecraft and diplomacy that we have the power to knit together the gaps that emerge in every human society and, through statecraft and diplomacy, that we bridge the gulfs among the world's cultures. Mike Mansfield responded to that calling with a level of understanding and with a modesty and compassion that were unparalleled in his lifetime.

But I believe there is one dimension of what his extraordinary government career meant to him that can only be appreciated within the quiet of this sanctuary. "Whatever you do," says St. Paul, "do it in the name of our Lord Jesus Christ." "Whatever you did for one of these least brothers of mine, you did for me." For the Christian, it is the whole of human life, and not just religious and devotional works of prayer, that the Church believes can be sanctified. The profound influence and practice of the Church has always been to dignify, ennoble and transfigure in God the duties and opportunities apparent in every human life.

The great Jesuit scientist-theologian of the last century, Teilhard de Chardin, who did so much of his powerful research, as did Mike Mansfield, in the Far East, graphically yet simply expressed this Christian vision of human life in saying that God is found not only in withdrawal from the world in prayer or meditation; God is "in some sort at the tip of my pen, my spade, my brush ... of my heart and of my thought. By pressing the stroke, the line ... on which I am engaged, to its ultimate natural finish, I shall arrive at the ultimate aim toward which my innermost will tends." If the City of God could be built through the scholar's pen, how much more so through Senator Mansfield's creativity in shaping the planks of anti-poverty and civil rights and health and education that contemporaries called the Great Society—how much more so in employing his remarkable understanding and sensitivity to bring into constructive dialogue and mutual enrichment the cultures of east and west.

Those who worked closest with Ambassador Mansfield never heard a word spoken in anger. But to me, the Christian measure of the man in relation to individuals close to him was in his lifelong love and devotion to his wife, Maureen.

At an age when most of us expect that our most heroic accomplishments are behind us, Senator Mansfield watched his wife's bright intelligence slip into the eclipse of disease. He chose to provide the form of care only he could provide—with a tenderness and love the very best of professionalism could not duplicate. The eulogy that he delivered in her honor one year ago in this same chapel matched in sentiment the depth and unstinting character of his loving care for her.

The great French philosopher of the 20th century, Gabriel Marcel, taught us that mature human love, either of husband for wife or child—or of God—is never a single commitment we make once and then are done with. It is never a commitment before which we can stand passive. Mature human love must always be a form of creative fidelity that we make forever new.

Through nine full decades of his life, this humble, generous, good man gave us an example of creative fidelity that proved he was—to his nation and to the world, as his family and colleagues always knew him to be—authentically heroic.

Michael J. Mansfield (1903–2001; LLD '71) was one of the United States Congress's most distinguished members. A member of the House of Representatives from 1943–53 and Senate from 1953–77, he was the longest serving majority leader in history, serving from 1961–77. He also served as U.S. ambassador to Japan from 1977–88 and received the Medal of Freedom in 1989.

John J. Griffin

November 3, 1998

*John quite simply gave substance to
the great mystery of Christian marriage that is a sign
and symbol of Christ's love for all of us.*

"If anyone would serve me let him follow
me; where I am there will my servant be."

JOHN 12

ON BRIGHT SUMMER days in New England, the trees are so abundantly green, that our constant danger is to take them for granted. But as leaves become precariously fewer in the fall, reds and yellows and browns emerge to stir our appreciation as never before.

Last Friday morning, in the full, beautiful color of his autumn, John Griffin let go of the world and the family he loved so much to go to God.

I am sure I speak for all of us in expressing our sincere sympathy to Rita, John's spouse and second self of 55 years. To Maryann and Cecilia and Alice and Kathryn and John and Dennis and Robert, and to your spouses and children— and not least, to Bob and Austin, who understood John as only brothers can. We know the depth of your loss, because we share it. We know your assurance he is with God because we share your faith and experienced John's goodness.

The geographic route that John followed over his 85 years was not a long one. Raised in Somerville's Magoun Square,

John received a scholarship to attend Boston College. A direct man even then, John asked the priest who admitted him how he would ever repay the gift. The response was—just make sure that someone else has the same opportunity as you. In his generosity, John never stopped giving back. A year out of college in 1936, John entered the fuel business, which he practiced for 46 years, until his retirement to the Cape in 1978. A leader in his business, John served his community through leadership in charitable and civic and religious organizations throughout the metropolitan region.

This day is not long enough to recount the memories that each of us have of our relationship with John Griffin. They are memories of an unswerving determination and of great good fun, memories of dedicated effort and of satisfying accomplishment and of pride; but most of all, memories of intense friendships and of thanksgiving for the goodness of life. And with every memory, the awareness that, if a problem existed, we knew that in John Griffin, we had someone on our side.

John was a direct man who defined himself unambiguously by what he gave himself unreservedly to: his faith, his family, his professional livelihood, his alma mater.

As a businessman, John's success in his 46-year career was not measured just by the sheer joy and pride he experienced in what he called the best business in the world, his "profession" of selling. With characteristic humor, John always said that, as a home fuel executive, "Anybody with a chimney is a prime prospect for me." The fact is that many healthy businesses exist today only because John shared his knowledge and expertise and the material wherewithal for survival to once-struggling small businesses. A full 20 years after his retirement from the business he had entered only a year out of college, his entire industry conferred on him its first Legends Award.

Indeed, from today's vantage point, one must reach back to John's green years to conjure up again his enthusiasm for business. His devotion to Rita and the children was a constant, in green years and in gold, the joy of his life and the inspiration to his most complete gift of self. In this, John quite simply gave substance to the great mystery of Christian marriage that is a sign and symbol of Christ's love for all of us, his Church, whom he loved in life and in death.

If selling was John's art, and family his life vocation, I can say with gratitude that Boston College—for 62 eventful years—was his avocation. In his last conversation with his son, John spoke of his determination to attend the Notre Dame game. His last thought of a wardrobe was to request his BC tie for the game. The truth of the matter is—as he so often heard his friend Speaker "Tip" O'Neill say—that John Griffin's was a unique role in nourishing the life of his alma mater. One of Boston College's most precious endowments is not its handsome buildings or material resources; it is the intense loyalty and dedication of its graduates. From the mid-'50s to the mid-'80s, there was no effort to kindle that flame in which John Griffin's infectious enthusiasm and good humor and persuasive leadership did not play a role. In my judgment, from the '50s through the '80s, John was the living link between generations of volunteer leaders.

The University has expressed its gratitude to John by the award of its highest academic honor; his fellow graduates by the conferral of their loftiest alumni award. Yet persons who love and are loved know that such honors are inadequate to what is in the heart of either.

John's was a blessedly long and happy life. It wound its way through many paths and encountered many crossroads. Yet, John's was a life that was all of a single piece. No one who ever knew him over his 85 years doubted that beneath the good humor and zest for life, beneath the persuasiveness and the generosity, John was not only serving you and me, he was following someone. For John took to heart the words of Christ that "unless a grain of wheat falls to the earth and dies, it remains—just a grain of wheat—but if anyone would serve me, let him follow me; for where I am there will my servant be. And if anyone serves me, him, the Father, will honor." May he rest in peace.

John J. Griffin (1913–98; A&S '35), an oil executive by vocation, was by avocation a lifelong volunteer and participant in the life of Boston College. President of the Alumni Association and highly instrumental in the 1957 creation of an expanded football stadium, he was awarded the McKenney Medal in 1962.

Albert J. Kelley

ST. IGNATIUS CHURCH—CHESTNUT HILL

December 14, 2004

This was a man able to locate all gyrations of modernity against a stable horizon of honesty and directness to himself and others.

AMONG ALL OF the dramatic changes that shape modern life, perhaps none so perfectly epitomizes the reality of modernity as does the exploration of space. It is rooted in the most sophisticated of technologies, in the power and precision of the most advanced engineering, in the mathematical projections of planetary geography, and, most of all, in the outermost bounds of human courage and imagination and creativity. Counterpoint to the incessant change that space represents is the firmness and consistency of human aspirations and hopes, the assurance and confidence of religious faith and the warmth and simplicity of love, the modesty and openness of life lived according to the Beatitudes.

My dear friends, we are gathered this morning to celebrate the life of Dr. Al Kelley, a man who, to me, combined in his life all of the forward-looking excitement and sophistication of modern science and engineering with the modesty and humility and confident assurance and large-hearted love that comes with deeply held Christian faith.

I am sure that I speak for everyone in the congregation in extending my sympathy to Al's sons and their families, to

Mark and Shaun and David, and to his sister, Joanne and brother, Paul.

Al meant much to Boston College at a critical time in the University's history and in the history of its School of Management.

From the late '60s to the late '70s, every university in America experienced some of the most soul-searching challenges to their purpose and to their very way of life. Schools of business were uniquely challenged to prove their worth to students who had grown skeptical of the value of business institutions when measured against the pressing social issues of war and race that were luring students out of classrooms onto picket lines. And in the hierarchy of academic disciplines, business was still emerging from its status of job training to that of professional discipline, indispensable to business leadership and decision making.

Al brought to those challenges not only the rigorous education of a naval officer, flyer, and engineer, but the professional experience of high-level management in the nation's space administration. Quite simply, he launched the redesign of both graduate and undergraduate programs based on professional standards and began the welcome transformation of the faculty on the same standards. The enviable reputation of today's Carroll School of Management faculty and the selectivity and enthusiasm of its student body are the direct result of the professional initiatives Dean Al Kelley began.

But Al's technical professionalism never swallowed up all of his life.

This was a man able to locate all gyrations of modernity against a stable horizon of honesty and directness to himself and others, of faith and hope and love of God he had learned here in his childhood, and carried into maturity as husband and father and colleague to his peers. The Al we admired spoke from expertise and experience that had been sharpened and given added purpose by the sincerity and integrity of his own hopes, the perspective of his religious beliefs, and by the love for God and his fellow men and women that gave ultimate meaning to all he did.

I have struggled to find a symbol or metaphor for the unique ability Al had of smoothly meshing his deepest human and religious ideals with the outer reaches of his modernity.

A navy test pilot travels at speeds and to heights that to most of us would be dizzying; at times, it is impossible to look outside to gain one's bearings. But the pilot always has an instrument that allows him to simulate the horizon he cannot see. Al's sense of God's presence and his Christian faith that he learned here where his mother and father brought him as a child, was the horizon against which he was able to plot every dizzying height to which he rose; the horizon against which he was able to measure every risk he undertook; it was the steady source that gave beauty to his every love.

As father and husband and brother and business leader and patriot and officer and friend, Al, we salute you, we admire you, and most of all we are grateful to God for all He made you.

Albert J. Kelley (1924–2004), a Naval Academy graduate, came to Boston College from a career as naval pilot and NASA manager. Dr. Kelley served as dean of the School of Management (1967–78) and subsequently pursued a distinguished career in business, government, and education.

Thomas P. O'Neill Jr.

ST. JOHN THE EVANGELIST CHURCH—CAMBRIDGE,
MASSACHUSETTS

January 10, 1994

*Speaker O'Neill was large-hearted in
his every approach to the world around him.*

Your eminence, Cardinal Law; President Ford; President Carter; Vice President Gore and members of the Cabinet; Ambassador Flynn; Governor Weld; Members of the Congress and the Massachusetts Great and General Court; Mayor Menino; Mayor Reeves; Mrs. O'Neill (Millie); members of the O'Neill family; and my dear friends.

Our human family's loves and its losses have taught us many ways of expressing grief. In the clear, cold air of this weekend, flags flew at half-staff in the nation's Capitol and here at home. The Speaker's Chair in the House of Representatives wore a mantle of black. Silent lines of people, plain and powerful, filed into the State House. If there are times when symbols and individual physical presence to each other are more expressive than words, surely this is such a time. Mrs. O'Neill (Millie), Susan and Rosemary, Tom and Michael and Kip, the presence of each person here this morning is an expression of deepest respect and esteem for Speaker O'Neill; but it is even more an effort to ease your grief because we respect you so much in your sorrow and because your grief is ours as well.

On Wednesday evening, the Speaker wearily told Tom of the irresistible tiredness over him and peacefully closed his eyes for the last time. His sleep awakened not only the brilliance of the nation's writers; they responded with their hearts as well. Every step along the upward route of his public career has been carefully retraced. But it was clearly the man himself—in his humor and his inexhaustible desire to help, his courage and his compassion and his sheer goodness— that came through to his chroniclers and inspired them to masterfully faithful portraits that those who loved him will always cherish.

Those portraits I will not attempt to re-create this morning. There is, however, one feature of the background in each of those portraits that perhaps could not have been painted in, until this morning—in this sacred place. Every captivating account of the Speaker's momentous achievements in public life, of his easy familiarity with the world's great leaders, remarked that he never lost touch with his roots. And this was no mere metaphor. Those roots remained the source of his lifeblood and his identity as a person to the very end. The friendships of Barry's Corner, his love for Boston College, the comfortable streets of North Cambridge were as much a part of him as were his Speaker's gavel and his intense loyalty to his staff and colleagues in the Congress. But perhaps older than any of these—this parish, to which he returned this morning, has been a figure in the background of every change in family and political fortunes. It is not just a matter of ritual that in this parish he received the name of Thomas Junior at baptism; before this altar as a young man he knelt with Millie to pronounce their marriage vows; and for 35 years in the Congress, he returned humbly to reaffirm his worship that God was his origin and his destiny and that what he did with his enormous talents and his opportunities mattered to God as well. The truth is that God was as real to Speaker O'Neill as were you or I.

The role that faith plays in any of our lives is as elusive to describe as it can be powerful and pervasive. It was not something that Speaker O'Neill often put into language. (He was not a man given to self-explanation, but to action.) And yet faith was a recognizable dimension of everything he did in public and in private life. It was never a badge or an ornament to make others uncomfortable, but always a star he checked before setting his own course. Nor was his understanding of faith ever woodenly fixed, incapable of growth and development. Those of us who have lived through the decades since the '30s of dramatic change in the moral dilemmas that modernity brings, in the crises of wars and threats of war, in more nuanced understanding of our own religious convictions—those of us who have lived through these changes realize that Speaker O'Neill's legendary sense of loyalty, either to old friends or to God, was no dull or wooden conformity. It has been a creative fidelity to values pledged in his youth that he kept relevant to a world of constant change by dint of effort and imagination and at the cost of personal sacrifice.

What did the Speaker gain from his faith? A vantage point that gave him lifelong perspective on himself and his relationship to the world around him.

One of the most important ingredients to a portrait or to a human life is perspective—a sense of priority and of proportion among the parts. Over the past several days, countless commentators have remarked upon the extraordinary balance Speaker O'Neill maintained within an almost limitless range of commitments. Indeed, his spontaneous enthusiasm could easily have swept away any sense of proportion or perspective. For Speaker O'Neill was large-hearted in his every approach to the world around him. He was large-hearted in his compassion and in his humor; large-hearted in his understanding of people; large-hearted in his love of all things human, from family and friends to work and politics and sports. To Speaker O'Neill, everything was important—but nothing was so important that it was worth sacrificing fairness to one in need of a favor to a friend or the honor and integrity he owed God.

How many stories have been told and retold of Speaker O'Neill's walking with royalty but never losing perspective on himself or on every person he befriended. Each of those stories recognized that leadership in high public office invariably confers power and power has a potent magic to twist perspective and turn the heads of those who hold it. Speaker O'Neill possessed the antidote to that powerful magic. He did not frame it in abstruse theological language, but in the simple realization in faith of who he was and where he came from. He lived it in his unwavering sense of gratitude for his roots—in his recognition that his most valuable traits were gifts from family and friends and teachers and fellow workers—and ultimately were gifts of God Himself. And for the person who knows his roots, for the person who knows gratitude, power and high position and large-hearted love pose no dangers. They are, rather, even more effective instruments to be of service to the least.

The luminous sketches of the Speaker that have appeared this week are almost complete. In the foreground stands a grateful commonwealth and a grateful nation of countless individuals who owe their job, their education, their citizenship, indeed, their life to the friendship or the wisdom or the simple encouragement of this great man. In the background of the portrait stands the Christ, the measure of his own self-understanding and of his unabashed humility and the guarantor of the infinite importance of everything he did for the least of those he met.

But there is one more stroke of the brush that has been left unnoticed. If the Speaker's faith gave him perspective, the love of a great woman gave him the confidence that he could do whatever the nation or whatever God asked. The pride of the Speaker's life was not the Medal of Freedom nor the Legion of Honor; it was the love of his beloved Millie who gave courage to his struggles and measure to his success and loving understanding through his illness.

Those of us who live among the terraces of mountains are too close to their grandeur to take an accurate measure of their height. And during these many years you and I have known him and all of the staff and colleagues he esteemed so highly, have been like those individuals so familiar with their landscape that we are unable to grasp its dramatic proportions. But this morning, with the gavel finally silent, and the last story told, and the last anxious heart put at ease, we now know that his stature rose higher than all the rest. And we know the blessing of having known him as a friend and we ask only that his generous soul enjoy the presence of the Risen Lord, whom he worshipped.

Thomas P. O'Neill Jr. (1912–94; A&S '36; LLD '73), Speaker of the House of Representatives (1977–87) and a Boston College trustee (1972–87), was the recipient of the McKenney Award in 1964 and Ignatius Medal in 1981. From his graduation in 1936 to his election to the highest national office of any Boston College graduate, Speaker O'Neill assured that his own growth to national stature enhanced the stature of his alma mater as well.

CHAPTER V

HAPPENINGS
ALONG THE WAY

Introduction

THE SOCIAL UPHEAVALS that broke through campus gates between 1968 and 1972 dispelled whatever traces still lingered from the myth of the university as an ivory tower. The pressing issues of race, of poverty, and of war not only became topics of passionate interest on campus, they became chasms that divided University clienteles and ironically made the University itself the target of frustrated energies.

Of the three, the Vietnam War generated by far the most intense demonstrations of passionate feeling. By the time of my arrival at Boston College in the fall of 1972, the flood tide of feeling had ebbed and the Paris Peace Accord of January 1973 was a signal that chasms could be bridged and older priorities of education and civility could be restored.

Yet the experience of 1968 to 1972 had definitively shattered the splendid isolation rightly or wrongly considered a prerogative of universities. University leaders recognized that their institutions enjoyed all of the prerogatives—and responsibilities—of authentic citizenship in their local community, in their nation, and in their world. They had a distinctive contribution to make not only through the lives of their graduates, but through their own powerful resources. And as reservoirs of intelligence and of research, they had an obligation to provide perspective on the complexities of the world around them.

As the first liberal arts college founded in the city of Boston, Boston College was long known to many as "Boston's college." When the city, in 1954, was experiencing its deep depression of economic stagnation and decadelong lack of construction, Boston College, with its Citizen Seminars, was recognized as the only broker that could bring together business and government and advocacy groups to reignite initiative and begin the long process of rebuilding. But Boston College is a citizen of many worlds. It is kindred institution not only to the distinguished company of Greater Boston's colleges and universities, but is sister to the 27 other Jesuit universities in the U.S. and scores of those abroad. Indeed, even the College's managerial "rags to riches" history of the past 30 years provided lessons helpful to others undergoing the same experience.

During the 24 years I served as president of Boston College, I took as one of my responsibilities to assure Boston College's continuing contributions to the many communities in which we enjoy membership. This final selection of talks represents only a handful of occasions to reflect on one or other facet of the College's relationship to its larger world.

Heisman Trophy Dinner

NEW YORK HILTON

December 6, 1984

*Doug Flutie . . . gave coast-to-coast televised
demonstration . . . of what education of the complete
person can be.*

THE HEISMAN TROPHY is not conferred upon a college
or university, upon a coach or university faculty member.

It is an honor bestowed directly upon an individual student
who has been judged for that year the best player in the land.

And yet, in receiving the Heisman award, Doug Flutie has
brought genuine honor to Boston College—because Doug so
clearly represents not only the excellence we strive for in our
athletic teams, but he personifies just as sincerely the ideals
of a talented and dedicated student and the ideals of personal
character that Boston College values so highly.

A university does not create intelligence or athletic ability
or virtue or character. It prays for the insight to recognize
them in its students; it is thankful for them; and it attempts
to muster the best tools available to assist them to follow
its vision of what the fully educated person can be: a vision
that includes the unfolding of mind and heart and will and
imagination.

For more than a century, Boston College has thought of
its collegiate education as forming not only the mind but the
complete person—mind and heart and will and imagination. Then along came Doug Flutie and in his modest but

very dramatic way, gave coast-to-coast televised demonstration—off the field and on—of what education of the complete person can be.

In so doing, he is a source of great pride to Boston College. He adds genuine distinction to intercollegiate football and to this 50th anniversary of the Heisman Trophy Award.

It is rare that a university president has the opportunity, in the presence of a young man's parents and thousands of his friends, to express his pride and sincere admiration for one of his own students. That opportunity is mine tonight. Boston College and I are immensely proud of this young man. We feel ourselves blessed to have had a part in developing some of his extraordinary gifts of person. We shall follow his career wherever it leads him—with pride and much affection and with sincere prayers for continued blessings.

Dr. Kenneth G. Ryder

PRESIDENT OF NORTHEASTERN UNIVERSITY

April 12, 1986

There is something beyond intelligence
that a president must bring to his office. He must have a deep
and abiding belief in his institution—a belief in its
integrity and worth and value.

Several weeks ago, at a dinner honoring Speaker O'Neill on March 17, President Reagan said that he understood the reason why he had been invited to speak at the testimonial was because Tip wanted someone on the dais who had actually met St. Patrick. Though I'm not quite a contemporary of President Reagan, there are members of the audience tonight who will recall that 10 years ago I had the privilege of speaking at the testimonial honoring President Asa Knowles as he was closing out his tenure and preparing a way for the inauguration of Ken Ryder.

The same sense of respect and admiration and of genuine friendship that animated my remarks on that occasion bring me back to the microphone to express a few words of appreciation for President Ryder on behalf of the higher educational community.

Greater Boston has a unique perspective on the tremendous diversity that exists among institutions of higher education. For that reason, we in Greater Boston have a special understanding of the great variety of services that colleges and universities are equipped to provide to individual students, to our surrounding communities, to neighboring business enterprises, and indeed, to the human family that constantly seeks to create new knowledge and explores new values in order to fashion the cultural home in which we find our fulfillment.

In a very real sense, every university president becomes identified with the institution he heads, and in some small measure the institution is identified, in many peoples' eyes, with its president. In the case of Ken Ryder, that identification has been a source of energy and stimulus and commitment; on the part of Northeastern it is a reason for very genuine pride. Anyone who has watched the higher educational scene is aware that different times call for differing forms of leadership. As American society changed, university presidents have successively been scholars and diplomats and managers and fundraisers, as the occasion demanded. But there are three characteristics that I believe every president needs to successfully lead a major institution. He or she needs a gift of understanding broad enough to grasp the enormous complexity involved in the conduct of these burgeoning institutions. But no degree of sheer intelligence will make an effective leader. He must have that art of practical judgment that is key to the decisions that are the fuel if these large institutions are to move and adapt and change and go forward. But practical judgment, too, is a form of intelligence, and there is something beyond intelligence that a president must bring to his office. He must have a deep and abiding belief in his institution—a belief in its integrity and worth and value to the people it benefits—that will stand strong against the obstacles and disappointments and misunderstandings that are inevitable in every human enterprise worth one's commitment.

Ken Ryder has displayed that he not only understands but is totally at home in the largest private university in the world. By instinct, he is unambiguous and clear and decisive.

I suppose my most frequent contacts with Ken are a result of his unremitting efforts to use the educational resources of Northeastern for the benefit of the city of Boston, and to bring the university's name to the leadership of the National Association of Independent Colleges and Universities, that he chairs this year. And yet I realize that these off-campus activities are only possible because of his belief in the fundamental mission of his University in making a sound education available to thousands of young men and women whose lives will never quite be the same because of their experience, and who will make the world better because of the education they have received.

The Most Reverend
Peter-Hans Kolvenbach

SUPERIOR GENERAL OF THE SOCIETY OF JESUS

October 5, 1988

*You evoke the memory of an unbroken line of individual
Jesuits and lay colleagues who communicated
those ideals [of Jesuit education].*

Reverend Father General, on behalf of the Boston College community of faculty and students and of our 100,000 living alumni, I am honored to welcome you to our campus. To all of you, graduates of Boston College High School and of Boston College, I am grateful for joining us in welcoming Father General to our midst.

Even during a 125th anniversary year, it is rare that a single evening has the power to recapitulate a lifetime of an institution. But the presence of each of you makes this gathering just such an evening for Boston College and for Boston College High School.

Despite the freshness of the walls and corridors in this new building, echoes from other halls and classrooms on Harrison Avenue are strong among us. Indeed, the ground on which we stand tonight and the towers of our academic buildings on the Heights, are each successive milestones in the history of this University that were set in place, Father General, with the guidance and assistance of one of your predecessors.

Your presence this evening, therefore, and the office you

exercise, represent the distinctive inspiration that the name "Jesuit" has meant to this University over the past 125 years: the challenge to give freely what we have freely received; the exercise of personal care for individual students; and above all, that humbling challenge of fashioning an education not only representative of the best of the worlds of intelligence and culture, but an education that enriches and is enriched by a personal faith and hope and love in Christ the Lord.

In your office as General, you evoke in this audience, however, more than recollection of the ideals of Jesuit education. You evoke the memory of an unbroken line of individual Jesuits and lay colleagues who communicated those ideals. If each individual in this room who is a graduate of Boston College and Boston College High School could personally speak, I am sure that most would link their dedication to these institutions to an individual Jesuit or lay colleague who played a singular part in their academic achievement or their personal development or the maturing of their religious faith. Perhaps this association of a university with individual persons is a common phenomenon. But I believe it is especially true of Jesuit schools and universities, because their unique mission in serving both the advancement of human culture and the deepening of union with God is a synthesis only fully realized in the life of individual persons.

Among our number tonight, reaching back to the '30s and the '20s—we have leaders in medicine and law, in education and business, persons who have shaped the American Church and every branch of civil government. But they bring with them to this gathering memories of that long line of individuals who shaped their lives in irreversible ways—a Fr. John McCarthy and a Michael Walsh, an Alice Bourneuf and a Sandy Jenks, a Henry McMahon and a Fr. Joseph Shea. To our thousands of graduates, persons like these were Boston College, and personified that mysterious relevance of faith to human culture and of every facet of human culture to Christian faith. At times they spoke this relevance; perhaps more often they left it unspoken. But through the integrity of their lives, they stimulated young, observant minds to forge for themselves a life of distinguished service to God and to their surrounding world. And tonight, in these new halls, in your presence, we celebrate 125 years of those accomplishments.

Father General, I realize that in your travels you do not accept physical mementos of your visits to individual institutions. I would, however, like to commemorate your honoring us during our 125th anniversary by establishing some lasting recognition of your visit.

As you know, the Jesuits of the New England Province have served the people of the island of Jamaica for many decades. St. George's College in Kingston, Jamaica, is a Jesuit school that currently serves some 1,200 students, most of whom live in unspeakable poverty. Perhaps the school's most important asset in providing a strong education that will lift these young people from their poverty is a principally lay faculty of some 60 persons. Boston College tonight is creating a program of Kolvenbach Scholars that will bring young members of the St. George's faculty to Boston College where they will gain their advanced degrees. We trust that this initiative will not only extend Boston College's educational efforts to serve the advancement of faith and justice in assistance to the poor, but that it will also recollect some facets in the pursuit of your own vocation as priest and scholar and teacher.

Fr. Peter-Hans Kolvenbach entered the Society of Jesus in his native Netherlands and became a scholar in general linguistics and Oriental languages. From 1968 to 1981, he served as professor of linguistics and of Oriental languages at the Institute of Oriental Languages in Beirut and at St. Joseph's University in Beirut, before becoming provincial of the Middle East region of the Jesuits in 1981. Fr. Kolvenbach later became rector of the Pontifical Oriental Institute in Rome, and in 1982 was elected General of the Society of Jesus.

John McElroy

PRESIDENT'S CIRCLE ADDRESS

May 19, 1991

*This was a giant of a man, in his talent, in his stamina, in his
vision—a man who was denied education in his own life and made it
possible for tens of thousands of others.*

I HAVE OFTEN FELT there is a message in the seasons. For
the past 18 years, we have been gathering on Commencement
eve, amid the first pale colors of spring—as our young graduates felt the stirrings of new beginnings and the University
itself experienced again the exhilaration of youth. This year,
spring has ripened, not to the monotony or dryness of high
summer, but to the rich colors of hopes already realized but
newly promising.

I have the sense that Boston College this year is experiencing the robust vigor of spring fully in bloom, of youth
sensing the confidence of early maturity. And, of course,
none of us, neither individual men or women, nor colleges
and universities, reach maturity on our own. And that is
one reason why it is so appropriate that we gather at the
close of the year in the President's Circle. Because it is you
and those of your number not with us this evening that
have provided the strong hand that eased our way through
the uncertainties of the early springtime of this University.

Four days ago, I had the wonderful privilege of receiving an
honorary doctorate in civil and canon law from University
College Cork in Ireland. The former prime minister, Garrett

FitzGerald, had nominated me for the degree and, despite the highly unfortunate timing of the event, I felt it important to Boston College that I accept.

The Irish in Ireland are a direct people; and if in the president's and chancellor's introductory remarks there were some mildly laudatory remarks directed at me, they made it very clear that in honoring the president of Boston College, they were really honoring Boston College, and honoring it not for its splendid architecture or any of its individual scholars or programs, but for its distinguished performance of its high educational purpose.

And it is an occasion such as this that encourages us to focus not on individual buildings or projects, however new, or individual accomplishments, or even individual problems, however vexing.

Tonight is a night to celebrate, not the trees, but the forest, the high purpose and accomplishments of university education in the grand sweep. In Boston College's case, that sweep extends 128 years, and it has not only carried individuals and families forward, it has transformed their lives—professionally, culturally, and religiously.

On this night, I would like to go back for a moment to the beginning of that history to the person of John McElroy who founded Boston College, and who planted the seeds of the entire forest. When I had my opportunity to speak a few words in Ireland last week, I indicated that in honoring Boston College, University College Cork was honoring him. He was so remarkable a man that he deserved in his native country, and he deserves familiarity and pride from all of us, who have had a hand in advancing what he began.

John McElroy had his birthplace in Northern Ireland in 1782. Because of the religious strictures placed on Catholics at that time, he was allowed the opportunity of only two to three years of schooling. In 1803, he took ship to the states and, as soon as the suppression of the Jesuit Order was relieved in 1806, John McElroy became a Jesuit lay brother at the newly established Georgetown College. Indeed, it was from the windows of Georgetown that he watched the burning of Washington in the War of 1812. In his nine years of doing a variety of modest tasks at Georgetown, his intellectual talents became apparent, and he was invited to study for the priesthood. After only two years of theology he was ordained and became an almost instant success as a preacher and retreat-giver. Years after he gave a retreat to the priests in New York City, the cardinal called him back to the city to minister to him in his last illness. For a period of 23 years, he was stationed in Frederick, Maryland, and established there the largest Jesuit center in America—a magnificent church, the first consecrated west of Baltimore that remains splendid today, a school for boys and one for girls, a center where all young Jesuits received their early training until 1903. In 1846, the president of the United States requested John McElroy to be one of the original two Catholic chaplains to the United States Army that was then fighting in the Mexican-American War. After the war, he was sent to Boston and spent 10 full years struggling with the financial and political and religious obstacles to founding his college. The unrelenting vigor of his activities belied the fact that when John McElroy received the charter from the Great and General Court establishing Boston College in 1863, he was a man 81 years old. Though initially named president by his colleagues, he preferred that another carry on the work and he returned for the last 14 years of his life to Frederick, Maryland, to assist in the religious development of the newly entering Jesuits.

This was a giant of a man, in his talent, in his stamina, in his vision—a man who was denied education in his own life and made it possible for tens of thousands of others. Although Boston College from the beginning welcomed students from every national background, the difference Boston College made to the children of immigrants from his own country was revolutionary. From them and for the thousands who increasingly joined them from other backgrounds, we have some sense of the power and value of education. It works its wonders silently and over time; it gives eyes to see the world as the world never appeared, and it gives hands to do in the world what had never before been dreamed of.

That type of transformation took place again over the past four years in the young men and women who will graduate tomorrow. The effect is permanent, as it has been with all of you who preceded them.

That is why I wanted to accept the admiration for Boston College from an Irish university, and to accept it in the name of Fr. John McElroy. Our world would have been far different without him.

But there is one more part to Fr. McElroy's story. There has been much said during this Ignatian Year about the educational apostolates of Jesuits. But we are a long distance to-night from this man born two centuries ago, watching brick placed on red brick, on James Street, for the original Boston College. The college covered that distance, not through the efforts of Fr. McElroy but through you, and the others before you whose full partnership in those efforts have made them succeed, and made them revered. So whether you knew it or not, on Tuesday of this week along with Fr. John McElroy, you were in the great hall in University College Cork being honored for what you have accomplished in education at Boston College.

Tomas Cardinal O'Fiaich

HONORARY DEGREE CEREMONY

October 23, 1981

*I would hope that the genius of the Irish people
that animates your scholarship and your religious leadership
to all Ireland may continue to be the
genius of Boston College.*

YOUR EMINENCE, CARDINAL Medeiros; Your Eminence, Cardinal O'Fiaich; Monsignor Olden, director of St. Patrick's College of Maynooth.

It is for me a very distinct honor and singular pleasure to welcome Your Eminence, Cardinal O'Fiaich, to Boston College.

We stand today under the approving eye of St. Patrick, in the room that is called from the Gaelic citation on the rear wall, The Irish Hall of Boston. We stand in a room that has echoed with the voices of great Irish professors of years past, a Harney, a Murphy, a Connolly, a Walsh, giving testimony to the debt we owe to Irish culture and proud that in some measure we have been able to extend the riches of Irish culture, talent, and ideals to our own beloved America.

Boston College, that now enjoys the largest full-time student body in the Catholic sector of higher education, is perhaps the only university in the United States that was originally founded for the education of children of Irish immigrants. Fr. McElroy, who was the founder of Boston College, was born in 1782 in the same town of Brookeborough whence came the forebears of our honored guest, Cardinal O'Fiaich.

Boston College therefore owes its origin to the desire and aspiration for education on the part of Irish who came in such extraordinary numbers to this city; and in turn, Boston College became the focus, the beacon of their intellectual aspirations. I believe that the measure of the early success of this institution lay in our capacity, not to turn an ethnic culture in upon itself, but rather to recognize the faith and talent and ideals of its students as treasures to be enhanced in order to make their contribution to the entire culture of our Church and our country.

We honor you today, Cardinal O'Fiaich, as scholar, as churchman, and as native of Ireland—all three characteristics that resonate with the history of this institution and with the ideals of our present.

In honoring you today, I would hope that the genius of the Irish people that animates your scholarship and your religious leadership to all Ireland may continue to be the genius of Boston College, namely, a fascination with the power and the richness of language and of song; a respect for the brilliance of intelligence even more than its capacity for controlled and methodic scholarship; an asceticism of mind and heart that is as much a condition of scholarship as it is of sanctity; an abiding faith that enhances appreciation of all things human, but recognizes that the ground of their beauty lies beyond them; and lastly, a tangible sense of community and of oneness that links us together in the oneness of Christ's humanity we share.

The Partnership

10TH ANNIVERSARY GALA

November 20, 1997

*We know that we see the world best and
appreciate it most when we see it through shared eyes.*

ANYONE WHO SERVES a full 24 years as a president of a
modern university inevitably becomes the recipient of an occasional honor or award. I have always retained the salutary
recognition that such awards are given more out of respect
for the institution one represents, rather than the individual
chosen. Tonight's honor, however, will always be one that I
singularly appreciate.

It is bestowed by an organization, The Partnership, that is
wholly positive in its purpose. In enlarging the presence of
persons of color in the business and professional communities of Boston, it has succeeded not only in expanding the careers of talented individuals; it has immensely enriched the
business and professional and governmental life of the city.

Ten years ago, we did a survey that determined that
among the extraordinarily dedicated African-American
students who came to Greater Boston's renowned graduate and professional schools, few even considered launch-
ing their professional careers in our city. Thus was born the
program called The Boston Fellows. Now, each year there

is a carefully crafted program that introduces young black professionals beginning their careers here to the culture and institutions and government bodies and social life of the city of Boston.

Most of us think of the learning process, the process of becoming familiar with new surroundings, as an individual achievement. But in fact, we know that we see the world best and appreciate it most when we see it through shared eyes. The most striking meeting of each year's Fellows is the first meeting of the year, when new Fellows from Framingham and the North Shore, and Scituate and the South End meet each other for the first time and the overwhelming reaction is, "I didn't know that you were here."

In learning the city together, through shared eyes, they come to appreciate the city and that appreciation releases their own store of talents to enrich the life of Boston.

It is my profound respect for the Partnership, whose reality mirrors its name, that makes this award a source of sincere gratitude.

Dr. Martin Luther King Jr.

KING DAY HOLIDAY OBSERVANCE

January 15, 1981

*He profoundly appreciated the religious worth
of people; and he profoundly appreciated
human freedom.*

I HAVE LOOKED FORWARD very much to talking to you today because this memorial is doubly instructive to us. We look back to Martin Luther King today recalling not simply the accomplishments of a human life, but also the motivation and the ideals that were the inspiration for those accomplishments. And, as always, the ideals of a person transcend the time in which he or she lived, and are forces that can motivate us, as well as the person that we memorialize.

With so much being written in the press today about his achievements as an orator, a writer, as a religious leader, as a social leader of his people, I will not direct my own remarks to the events of Martin Luther King's life. But I believe even more important than the individual accomplishments of his life were the ideals and aspirations that motivated him.

I would like to single out three values that I know he considered extremely important. They are equally important to us today.

Martin Luther King was a person who profoundly appreciated knowledge; he profoundly appreciated the religious worth of people; and he profoundly appreciated human freedom. I want to say just a word about each of these.

Especially as a University, I think we should be acutely aware of the importance of mind, and the importance of learning to Martin Luther King. He invested the greater part of his own too short life in formal education. He was a well-educated person, educated for his final degree in our own city, as you know, at Boston University. The long article on the second page of *The Boston Globe* today contains a comment about one interesting aspect of his regard for the importance of learning. It is also an example of his gift of brief and graphic expression. He said that it would be impossible for our hearts long to be right if our heads were wrong. He recognized the importance of knowing, the importance of learning, not only for itself, but also for the enlightenment it provides to the human heart. I am convinced today that there is nothing more important to equality for all races in this country than education and the knowledge it brings.

Secondly, Martin Luther King was a profoundly religious person whose appreciation of his fellow people had religious origins. He recognized each of them, each of us, as reflections of God whose creation we are, and also as brothers and sisters of Christ who have been redeemed by Him. He saw in human hardship constant symbols of the Crucifixion and of the Lord's suffering on the Cross. This is important because his religious appreciation of the dignity and worth of every individual person was the source both of his strength and of his charity, of his nonviolence. Because his appreciation of the worth of individual people was religious, he could be morally outraged as he was, and yet always moderate that moral outrage with charity towards others, in ways that were nonviolent.

Lastly the importance of freedom. I suppose as we watch television clips, the aspiration of his that strikes us most is that of freedom. "Free at last, Free at last!" Those powerfully delivered words of his are still ringing. Yet it is very important for us to recognize that for him, freedom was not just freedom *from*, whether from ignorance, or from economic oppression, or from any other type of slavery, but freedom to *do* things, freedom for fulfilling activity. Life is a type of activity, and there is only fulfillment in what we do. Freedom is important, therefore, in being not just a lack of constraint, but in being a capacity to do things, an openness and opportunity to use our powers. Again with typical pithiness, he said that what is important is not just freedom to sit on a bus, but that we learn to live with other people. Black people and white people, all of us have to have that freedom and that necessity—to learn to live with other people.

The freedom we all seek is freedom to pursue happiness. What is that elusive reality—happiness? What does it consist of? Everyone wants the freedom to pursue happiness, but what is it? It is at least the freedom to pursue fulfillment in family life, fulfillment in the world of work, fulfillment in exercising citizenship, fulfillment religiously. Those are the arenas of freedom that Martin Luther King was interested in—freedom for the pursuit of fulfillment within family, within country, within a world of work and profession, within a universe responsive to God.

Those three ideals, that of knowledge, of appreciation for one's religious worth, and the ideal of freedom were moving forces behind this extraordinary life of accomplishment. They should still be ideals for us, especially in this University that is dedicated to learning, that is religiously appreciative of individual people and dedicated to freedom.

What would I hope for Boston College on Martin Luther King Day? I hope for two things. My aspiration for Boston College is that there be no institution in the Greater Boston area, in the state of Massachusetts, where black people are more welcome as students, as staff, as faculty members, than they are at Boston College. That would be my aspiration for two reasons. First I would hope that no institution is superior to Boston College in appreciating humanistically the importance of every individual person, the importance of human mind, the importance of human heart, the importance of human spirit. Furthermore, I would hope that no institution's welcome to minority students should be warmer because Boston College enjoys a religious vantage point that should enable us to recognize in the individuality of human mind, of human spirit, not just humanistic worth but a reflection of their Creator, and a destiny that is religiously compelling. Is it overly abstract to say that you love a person or are interested in people because of their reflection of something beyond them? The truth is that you can only really appreciate God if you can appreciate individual people; and you can appreciate individual people best if you can also appreciate and recognize them as bearers and reflections of the beauty and dignity beyond them.

Secondly, I would hope that each of us, of every color, of every race, of every nationality could benefit to the utmost from the presence of each to each other. Where we can benefit most, is not so much perhaps through expansion of each other's minds as through expansion of each other's hearts.

I had the valuable opportunity of spending some four years of my education in Europe and, though the cultural differences between America and Europe may not seem great, they can be very, very significant. To live for extended periods in French homes, and Flemish and German and Spanish homes, makes one acutely conscious of the cultural differences between yourself and others, and among those national cultures themselves. It's not so much that you see things differently, as that you appreciate things differently. In my first year overseas, I suspected that people I was with were, frankly, deluded in the things they appreciated. Second year I began to realize it was no delusion. In the third year the suspicion arises that Americans are the ones deluded, and the fourth year, you begin to put it all together—with an expanded heart. That is what we can do for each other—by learning through each other not only intellectually, but in the heart's ways of appreciating.

Culturally there are many, many differences in this room. There are many, many differences in this University between people of the same race, between people of different races. We can learn from each to expand our hearts, to appreciate things others appreciate that have not been part of our familial culture. This is one of the great wealths, and great beauties of humanity, that there is such richness and diversity in cultural appreciation. That each of us enrich our own cultural appreciation by living among each other, learning from each other, expanding the sensitivities of each other's hearts, would be the second aspiration I entertain on Martin Luther King Day for Boston College.

Jesuit Murders in El Salvador

JOHN JOSEPH MOAKLEY VIGIL SERVICE AT
THE STATE HOUSE, BOSTON

May 31, 2001

*Why did a gruesome murder 3,000 miles away stir
Joe Moakley to what he considered his greatest accomplishment?*

"AMEN I SAY to you, whatever you did for one of these least brothers of mine, you did for me."

Both here in Boston and in the tiny Central American country of El Salvador, this is the final week of the Easter season, the season when Christ's death is still fresh in our memories, but when we celebrate in faith our confidence in newly risen life. In the three short days since Memorial Day, the word of Joe's passing has kindled not only the brilliance of the city's writers and its cameramen; it touched their hearts as well. Every step along the route of his public career, from the streets of South Boston to the halls of Washington, has been faithfully, even lovingly portrayed.

Those portraits I will not attempt to retrace this evening. I believe that there is one reason why Congressman Moakley suggested that I have the privilege of speaking this evening. Joe frequently and publicly said that of all the accomplishments that were his in over 40 years of public service, his proudest accomplishment was in bringing to light the truth about the atrocious murders of six Jesuit priest-educators and their housekeepers at the University of Central America in El Salvador. It was that thin but sharp ray of light that was the beginning of the return of peace and justice to that troubled land.

As one who stood on the ground in El Salvador during Joe's work there, I would like to re-create, as much as I can 10 years later, the circumstances that made what he did so important to the world and so proud an accomplishment to Joe. Why did a gruesome murder 3,000 miles away stir Joe Moakley to what he considered his greatest accomplishment?

The persons murdered were Jesuit priests and two of their housekeepers. People the world over, if they know of the existence of Jesuits, think of us as educators. But Jesuit education, especially at the University of Central America, has never pursued knowledge merely for its own sake, but always as a cultural force to bring about greater equality among people, as an instrument to improve the condition of the human family, to ease the oppression that comes from poverty, at times even the oppression of political leaders who use well-trained armies to enforce their oppression.

Such was the case in El Salvador in the decade of the '80s. As Ignacio Ellacuria, the murdered Jesuit president of the University of Central America expressed it:

> The reality of El Salvador, the reality of the Third World, that is, the reality of most of this world … is fundamentally characterized by the … predominance of falsehood over truth, injustice over justice, oppression over freedom, poverty over abundance, in sum, of evil over good … That is the reality with which we live … and we ask ourselves what to do about it in a university way. We answer …: We must transform it, do all we can to ensure that … freedom [predominates] over oppression, justice over injustice, truth over falsehood, and love over hatred. If a university does not decide to make this commitment, we do not understand what validity

it has as a university. Much less as a Christian-inspired university.

It was because of this message successfully being communicated that at one o'clock in the morning of November 16, 1989, a battalion of troops entered the campus of the Jesuit University in El Salvador, roused the Jesuit president and five of his brother professors from their sleep, forced them onto a little plot of grassy land behind their simple residence, and then dispatched them on the spot. They then proceeded to shoot up the surrounding buildings with machine guns to make the murders look as though they were perpetrated by guerrilla forces.

It all appears so clear-cut and transparent today. But when it happened, the Military High Command issued a statement declaring that it had been guerrillas that were responsible for the murders. The American Embassy, whose government had trained here in the States some of the very triggermen who committed those murders, pointed the finger of blame not at the military, but at the guerrillas.

In January of 1990, the Speaker of the House appointed Congressman Joe Moakley to an extraordinary, select committee to investigate the crimes in El Salvador. In some ways, that appointment changed Joe Moakley's life forever. But for all who knew him best, from the Speaker who appointed him to the former Speaker who encouraged him, that appointment simply tapped into the rich veins of faith and determination and courage, veins of optimistic hope and of care for those most in need that had been his since childhood.

Faith was not something that Joe wore on his sleeve or that made people uncomfortable, yet it was a perspective that he brought to everything he did in public and private life. It was a lifelong perspective on himself and on the people around him. In that perspective, he saw the inviolable dignity of every human person and the irresistible call of those in need; faith gave a new dimension to his sense of justice and of fairness; it made him unswerving when the powerful served themselves at the expense of the weak. It was this faith and his courage and sense of justice Joe Moakley brought to El Salvador.

The measure of Joe Moakley's faith and of his courage in carrying out his charge is the measure of the forces that opposed him—not a few ruthless individuals, but the U.S.-trained military establishment of a sovereign nation that could enforce silence on witnesses as effectively as it had committed murder. Perhaps most difficult of all, Joe also faced the embarrassing efforts of some of his own governmental colleagues to set false trails away from the guilty and to withhold keys to the truth that they themselves held.

There is no doubt but that the authoritative voice of one man and his courage to use it ultimately broke the dam of silence and kindled hope that peace and justice could again be realities. Within a year of his appointment, criminal investigations in El Salvador were raised to the level of full trials. For the first time in El Salvador's history, two military officers were convicted for their part in the crime. Within another year, peace accords were signed in the U.N. between the government and its warring opponents. And although those suspected of ultimately ordering the murders were never tried, and men who confessed to killing the university Jesuits were exonerated for acting under orders, the system of governmentally organized oppression and murder had been broken. Thanks to Joe, the truth had come to light; the nation itself has begun to taste the first fruits of peace. And in the light of that truth and that peace, a whole people have realistically begun to live again.

What made this story the greatest accomplishment of Joe's public life? It was its straight-line continuity with what Joe had done all his life. It simply played out on a world stage Joe's lifelong faith in the inviolable dignity of every human being, his unique sense of justice and fairness, and the unswerving courage he had always shown on behalf of those who were weak and in need. That was what Joe had been for 40 years in South Boston and in the halls of Congress, and most of all, it was what he had believed from the first time he heard the Gospel message in his parish church, "Whatever you did for one of these least brothers of mine, you did for me."

Yitzhak Rabin

*The loss of Yitzhak Rabin is a challenge to the oneness of
our world, a challenge to peace everywhere.*

T HERE ARE MANY forms of human love. Each involves
a subtle mix of respect and of admiration. And if the capacity to declare one's love, one's respect and admiration is the
measure of our fullness as human persons, it is also the expression of our deepest vulnerability. For the loss of one we
respect, one we admire, one we love is perhaps the deepest
wound we can experience. The love of one individual for another—and indeed the loss of one individual to another, of
wife for husband, of child for parent, is literally ineffable. It
cannot be spoken because its singularity cannot be captured
in the abstractions of language.

For the past three days we have witnessed and heard the
unspeakable struggles of a granddaughter attempting to find
words to express her love and loss of her grandfather. And we
have witnessed and heard the admiration and love and loss
of a nation for its leader, the respect and reverence and loss of
the entire human family for one of its most courageous and
daring protagonists of peace.

We at Boston College did not share the degree of personal
familiarity with Yitzhak Rabin that enflamed the wound of
loss experienced in Israel. But it is important that this University gather in solidarity with women and men and chil-

dren the world over in acknowledging our profound loss of one of our human family's great protagonists for peace.

We gather as a University community dedicated to the cultural advancement of our common destiny, not through the violent force either of words or physical power, but through the creative strength of intelligence in the spirit of cooperative goodwill that is necessary if any human enterprise is to go forward. Force will perhaps always masquerade as the ultimate resort to achieve even our loftiest goals, but the immediate purpose of violent words and deeds are not to build but to destroy.

If universities have a single message to teach at the end of the 20th century, it is that our world is one and that its many elements are daily more interdependent upon each other.

Devastating hunger in Rwanda impoverishes us all. Massive indignities in Bosnia wound the human person everywhere. If peace cannot be pursued in one part of the world, peace is not secure anywhere.

If love and admiration are the measure of our fulfillment, and loss of a loved one our deepest vulnerability, that loss is also our greatest challenge. The loss of Yitzhak Rabin is a challenge to the oneness of our world, a challenge to peace everywhere. But the oneness of our world is inevitable, the power of peace irresistible—because in rising to the challenge, we will make them so.

We stand, therefore, this afternoon in the presence of the God of Abraham, the God of Moses, who is also the God of Jesus Christ and of each of us in this audience, to commend to God's infinite mercy the soul of Yitzhak Rabin, this great protagonist for peace.

Distinguished American Award

NATIONAL FOOTBALL FOUNDATION

December 10, 1996

*It is an award that invokes what all
of us feel for America.*

O VER THE COURSE of two and a half decades as a university president, one almost inevitably becomes the recipient of occasional expressions of honor.

But tonight is very different. Tonight's award is not another academic honor or degree. It is an award that invokes what all of us feel for America.

My entire professional life has been in higher education. So while there is pride and gratitude in receiving the Distinguished American Award, I clearly recognize that my selection is not a tribute to an individual but is public recognition of the invaluable contributions our nation's colleges and universities make to the greatness of America.

I had the opportunity to do much of my own doctoral study abroad—in England and France and Belgium. And one of the most striking differences between college and university education in the United States and almost anywhere else in the world is not what takes place in the classroom, but in the educational importance that we place in activities outside the classroom—in athletics and other forms of extracurricular achievement. Our academic programs are second to none in the world. But we in America see higher education as not just a matter of academics but a matter of head and heart and hand that can only be addressed outside the classroom, in the theater, in community centers and on the playing field.

I am not going to attempt to spell out, even in highlight form, the contribution our colleges and universities have made to American life and the lives of our graduates. The remarkable fact, however, is that through the entire period of America's history that runs from the last decade of the 19th century through the first 75 years of the 20th, only less than 20 percent of our population gained a bachelor's degree. During those years our nation moved through wars and peace, economic booms and busts, through perhaps the most dramatic period of social and cultural change the world has ever experienced. And despite the small, almost constant fraction of our population educated through college, the research productivity and trained managerial skills and cultural depth were here to create the world's most advanced quality of life at home and to assume the responsibilities of leadership in the international community.

All of us realize that the story higher education writes in the America of the next century must be different. It is not just that the world of business and technology and industry and the professions have become more technically complex; the moral dilemmas and cultural currents have become so subtle that the benefits of higher education in our society must be extended more broadly.

This afternoon I had the privilege of attending lunch with the 16 young scholar-athletes whom the Foundation and the Hall of Fame are honoring tonight. Each of these remarkable young men spoke briefly about what football has contributed to their lives. In each of their remarks I was struck by the pervasive realization all of them possessed that they were, even among their classmates, the privileged few who were gifted with the talent and the opportunity to play. For my part, if several years in Europe taught me the distinctiveness of American education—these same years taught me, as no experience at home could have, the privilege of having been born an American.

ACKNOWLEDGMENTS

My special gratitude to my long-time incomparable secretary Bronwyn Lamont, to Bill Bole for his editorial wisdom and to cover photographer Gary Wayne Gilbert for assistance in recovering photos.